THE PRESIDENTS

Editor

Fred L. Israel

VOLUME 7

Richard M. Nixon 1969 – Bill Clinton

973
PRE

Grolier Educational

SHERMAN TURNPIKE, DANBURY, CONNECTICUT

The publisher gratefully acknowledges permission from the sources to reproduce photos that appear on the cover.

Volume 1
J. Adams – New York Historical Society
J. Monroe – Library of Congress

Volume 2
J. K. Polk; A. Jackson; J. Tyler – Library of Congress
J. Q. Adams – National Archives

Volume 3
U. S. Grant – National Archives
A. Johnson; Z. Taylor – Library of Congress

Volume 4
B. Harrison; W. McKinley; J. A. Garfield – Library of Congress

Volume 5
H. Hoover; W. G. Harding – Library of Congress
T. Roosevelt – National Archives

Volume 6
D. D. Eisenhower – Library of Congress
L. B. Johnson – White House

Volume 7
B. Clinton – The White House
R. Reagan – Bush/Reagan Committee
G. Bush – Cynthia Johnson, The White House

Volume 8
T. Roosevelt – National Archives
B. Clinton – The White House

JH

Published 1997 exclusively for the school and library market by Grolier Educational

Sherman Turnpike, Danbury, Connecticut

© 1997 by Charles E. Smith Books, Inc.

Set: ISBN 0-7172-7642-2
Volume 7: ISBN 0-7172-7649-X

Library of Congress number:
The presidents.

p. cm.
Contents: v. 1. 1789–1825 (Washington–Monroe) — v. 2. 1825–1849 (Adams–Polk)
v. 3. 1849–1877 (Taylor–Grant) — v. 4. 1877–1901 (Hayes–McKinley) — v. 5. 1901–1933 (T. Roosevelt–Hoover)
v. 6. 1933–1969 (F. D. Roosevelt–L. B. Johnson) — v. 7. 1969–1997 (Nixon–Clinton)
v. 8. Documents, suggested reading, charts, tables, appendixes

1. Presidents – United States – Juvenile literature.
[1. Presidents.]   96-31491
E176.1.P9175   1997   CIP
973.099 — dc20   AC

For information, address the publisher
Grolier Educational, Sherman Turnpike, Danbury, Connecticut 06816

Printed in the United States of America

Cover design by Smart Graphics

VOLUME SEVEN

CONTRIBUTORS

EDITOR

Fred L. Israel received his Ph.D. from Columbia University. He has written several books for young adults including *Franklin D. Roosevelt, Henry Kissinger,* and *Know Your Government: The FBI.* Dr. Israel is also the editor of *History of American Presidential Elections, 1789–1968, The Chief Executive: Inaugural Addresses of the Presidents from George Washington to Lyndon Johnson,* and *The State of the Union Messages of the Presidents of the United States.* His most recent book is *Running for President, The Candidates and Their Images,* a two-volume work with Arthur M. Schlesinger, Jr. and David J. Frent.

Dr. Israel is Professor, Department of History, The City College of the City University of New York.

CONTRIBUTORS

Donald C. Bacon is a Washington-based journalist specializing in the presidency and Congress. He served as staff writer of *The Wall Street Journal* and assistant managing editor of *U.S. News and World Report.* A former Congressional Fellow, he is the author of *Rayburn: A Biography* and *Congress and You.* He is coeditor of *The Encyclopedia of the United States Congress.*

Hendrik Booraem V received his Ph.D. from The Johns Hopkins University. He taught social studies at Strom Thurmond High School, South Carolina, for many years. He has been Adjunct Professor at Rutgers University, Camden, Alvernia College, Lehigh University, and the State University of New York at Purchase. Dr. Booraem is the author of *The Formation of the Republican Party in New York: Politics and Conscience in the Antebellum North, The Road to Respectability: James A. Garfield and His World, 1844–1852,* and *The Provincial: Calvin Coolidge and His World, 1885–1895.*

Thomas Bracken received his B.A. and M.A., summa cum laude, from The City College of the City University of New York. He is currently enrolled in the doctoral program there, and he is Adjunct Professor of History.

David Burner received his Ph.D. from Columbia University. He is Professor of American History at the State University of New York at Stony Brook. Among Dr. Burner's many publications are *John F. Kennedy and a New Generation, The Torch is Passed: The Kennedy Brothers and American Liberalism* (with Thomas R. West) and *The Politics of Provincialism: The Democratic Party in Transition, 1918–1932.* He is also the coauthor of *Firsthand America: A History of the United States.*

Gary Cohn received his M.A. in Popular Culture Studies from Bowling Green State University in 1980 and has completed course work towards the doctorate in American History at the State University of New York at Stony Brook. As an Adjunct Professor he has taught history at The City College of the City University of New York and creative writing and composition at the C.W. Post campus of Long Island University.

Richard Nelson Current is University Distinguished Professor of History, Emeritus, at the University of North Carolina, Greensboro and former President of the Southern Historical Association. Among Dr. Current's many books are *Speaking of Abraham Lincoln: The Man and His Meaning for Our Times, Lincoln and the First Shot, The Lincoln Nobody Knows, Lincoln the President: Last Full Measure,* and with T. Harry Williams and Frank Freidel, *American History: A Survey.*

James B. Gardner received his Ph.D. from Vanderbilt University. He has been Deputy Executive Director of the American Historical Association since 1986 and Acting Executive Director of that organization since 1994. Dr. Gardner was with the American Association for State and Local History from 1979 to 1986, where he served in a variety of capacities, including Director of Education and Special Programs. Among his many publications is *A Historical Guide to the United States.*

Anne-Marie Grimaud received her B.A. from the Sorbonne, Paris and her M.A. from the State University of New York at Stony Brook, where she is currently enrolled in the doctoral program in American History.

Douglas Kinnard graduated from the United States Military Academy and served in Europe during World War II. He also served in Korea and Vietnam and retired as Brigadier General. He then received his Ph.D. from Princeton University. Dr. Kinnard is Professor Emeritus, University of Vermont and was Chief of Military History, U.S. Army. Among Dr. Kinnard's books are *Ike 1890-1990: A Pictorial History, President Eisenhower and Strategy Management: A Study in Defense Politics,* and *Maxwell Taylor and The American Experience in Vietnam.*

Robert A. Raber received his J.D. from the Law School, University of California, Berkeley. He retired from law practice and received his M.A. from The City College of the City University of New York, where he is enrolled in the doctoral program.

Donald A. Ritchie received his Ph.D. from the University of Maryland. Dr. Ritchie is on the Executive Committee of the American Historical Association, and he has been Associate Historian, United States Senate for 20 years. Among his many publications are *Press Gallery: Congress and the Washington Correspondents, The Young Oxford Companion to the Congress of the United States,* and *Oxford Profiles of American Journalists.*

Robert A. Rutland is Professor of History Emeritus, University of Virginia. He was editor in chief of *The Papers of James Madison* for many years, and he was coordinator of bicentennial programs at the Library of Congress from 1969 to 1971. Dr. Rutland is the author of many books including *Madison's Alternatives: The Jeffersonian Republicans and the Coming of War, 1805-1812, James Madison and the Search for Nationhood, James Madison: The Founding Father,* and *The Presidency of James Madison.* He is editor of *James Madison and the American Nation, 1751-1836: An Encyclopedia.*

Raymond W. Smock received his Ph.D. from the University of Maryland. He was involved with the Booker T. Washington Papers Project for many years and was coeditor from 1975 to 1983. He was Historian, Office of the Bicentennial, U.S. House of Representatives. In 1983, he was appointed as the first Director of the Office of the Historian of the U.S. House of Representatives. Among the major publications of that office are *The Biographical Directory of the United States Congress, 1774-1989, Black Americans in Congress, 1877-1989,* and *Women in Congress, 1917-1990.*

Darren D. Staloff received his Ph.D. from Columbia University, and he was a Post-Doctoral Fellow at the Institute of Early American History and Culture. He has taught at the College of Staten Island, Columbia University, and the College of William and Mary. Dr. Staloff is currently Assistant Professor of American History, The City College of the City University of New York. He is the author of *The Making of an American Thinking Class: Intellectuals and Intelligentsia in Puritan Massachusetts.*

John Stern received his M.A. from the State University of New York at Stony Brook, where he is enrolled in the doctoral program. His thesis is on Eugene McCarthy and the Presidential Campaign of 1968.

Edmund B. Sullivan received his Ed.D. from Fitchburg State College. He was Principal, New Hampton Community School, New Hampshire, and he taught at the North Adams and Newton public schools in Massachusetts. Dr. Sullivan was Professor at American International College and University of Hartford, and he was the founding Director and Curator of the Museum of American Political Life, West Hartford Connecticut. He is the author of *American Political Ribbons and Ribbon Badges, 1828-1988, American Political Badges and Medalets, 1789-1892,* and *Collecting Political Americana.*

Linda S. Vertrees received her B.A. in History from Western Illinois University and her M.A. in Library Science from the University of Chicago. She has written several annotated lists of suggested readings including the one for *The Holocaust, A Grolier Student Library.*

Thomas R. West received his Ph.D. from the Columbia University. He is Associate Professor, Department of History, Catholic University. He is coauthor, with David Burner, of *The Torch is Passed: The Kennedy Brothers and American Liberalism* and *Column Right: Conservative Journalists in the Service of Nationalism.*

INTRODUCTION

No branch of the federal government caused the authors of the Constitution as many problems as did the Executive. They feared a strong chief of state. After all, the American Revolution was, in part, a struggle against the King of England and the powerful royal governors. Surprisingly though, much power was granted to the president of the United States who is responsible only to the people. This was the boldest feature of the new Constitution. The president has varied duties. Above all, he must take care that the laws be faithfully executed. And also according to the Constitution, the president:

- is the commander in chief of the armed forces;
- has the power to make treaties with other nations (with the Senate's consent);
- appoints Supreme Court Justices and other members of the federal courts, ambassadors to other countries, department heads, and other high officials (all with the Senate's consent);
- signs into law or vetoes bills passed by Congress;
- calls special sessions of Congress in times of emergency.

In some countries, the power to lead is inherited. In others, men seize power through force. But in the United States, the people choose the nation's leader. The power of all the people to elect the president was not stated in the original Constitution. This came later. The United States is the first nation to have an elected president—and a president with a stated term of office. Every four years since the adoption of the Constitution in 1789, the nation has held a presidential election. Elections have been held even during major economic disruptions and wars. Indeed, these elections every four years are a vivid reminder of our democratic roots.

Who can vote for president of the United States? The original Constitution left voting qualifications to the states. At first, the states limited voting to white and very few black men who owned a certain amount of property. It was argued that only those with an economic or commercial interest in the nation should have a say in who could run the government. After the Civil War (1861–1865), the Fourteenth (1868) and Fifteenth (1870) Amendments to the Constitution guaranteed the vote to all men over the age of 21. The guarantee was only in theory. The Nineteenth Amendment (1920) extended the right to vote to women. The Nineteenth Amendment was a victory of the woman's suffrage movement which had worked for many years to achieve this goal. In 1964, the Twenty-fourth Amendment abolished poll taxes—a fee paid before a citizen was allowed to vote. This tax had kept many poor people, both black and white, from voting in several Southern states. And, the Twenty-sixth Amendment (1971) lowered the voting age to 18. (See Volume 8 for the complete text of the Constitution.)

In 1965, Congress passed the Voting Rights Act; it was renewed in 1985. This law, which carried out the requirements of the Fifteenth Amendment, made it illegal to interfere with anyone's right to vote. It forbade the use of literacy tests and, most important, the law mandated that federal voter registrars be sent into counties where less than 50 percent of the voting age population (black and white) was registered. This assumed that there must be serious barriers based on prejudice if so few had registered to vote. Those who had prevented African Americans from voting through fear and threat of violence now had to face the force of the federal government. Immediately, the number of African American voters in Southern states jumped dramatically from about 35 percent to 65 percent. In 1970, 1975, and 1982, Congress added amendments to the Voting Rights Act which helped other minorities such as Hispanics, Asians, Native Americans, and

Eskimos. For example, states must provide bilingual ballots in counties in which 5 percent or more of the population does not speak or read English. Today any citizen over the age of 18 has the right to vote in a presidential election. Many would argue that this is not only a right but also an obligation. However, all states deny the right to vote to anyone who is in prison.

Who can be president of the United States? There are formal constitutional requirements: one must be a "natural born citizen," at least 35 years old, and a resident of the United States for 14 years. The Constitution refers to the president as "he." It was probably beyond the thought process of the Founding Fathers that a woman, or a man who was not white, would ever be considered. The Twenty-second Amendment (1951), which deals with term limitations, uses "person" in referring to the president, recognizing that a woman could serve in that office.

How is the president elected? Most Americans assume that the president is elected by popular vote and the candidate with the highest number wins the election. This is not correct and may surprise those who thought they voted for Bill Clinton, Robert Dole, or Ross Perot in 1996. In fact, they voted for Clinton's or Dole's or Perot's electors who then elected the president. In the United States, the voters do not directly select the president. The Constitution provides a fairly complex—and some argue, an outdated—procedure for electing the president. Indeed, the electoral system devised by the Framers and modified by the Twelfth Amendment (1804) is unique. The records of the Constitutional Convention (1787) are silent in explaining the origins of the electoral system, usually referred to as the Electoral College. The several Federalist papers (Nos. 68–71) written by Alexander Hamilton in defense of the electoral system omit any source for the idea.

Under the electoral system of the United States, each state has the number of electoral voters equal to the size of its congressional delegation (House of Representatives plus Senate). Every 10 years, the census, as required by the Constitution, adjusts the number of representatives each state has in the House of Representatives because of population growth or loss. Every state always must have two senators. In the presidential election of 1996, for example, New York State had 33 electoral votes, because New York has 31 representatives and two senators. Alaska had three electoral votes, because Alaska has one representative and two senators. Since every congressional district must be approximately equal in population, we can say that the entire population of Alaska—the largest state in geographic size—is approximately equal in population to the 19th congressional district of New York City which covers the upper part of Manhattan Island.

There are 435 members of the House of Representatives. This number was fixed in 1910. There are 100 members of the Senate (50 states x 2 senators). This equals 535 electors. The Twenty-third Amendment (1961) gives the District of Columbia, the seat of our nation's capital, the electoral vote of the least populous state, three. So, the total electoral vote is 535 plus three or 538. To be elected president, a candidate must receive a majority, that is more than 50 percent, of the electoral votes: 270 electoral votes. If no candidate obtains a majority, the House of Representatives must choose the president from the top three candidates with each state delegation casting one vote. This happened in the 1824 presidential election. (See the article on John Quincy Adams.)

How does a political party choose its presidential nominee? Political parties play a crucial role—they select the candidates and provide the voters with a choice of alternatives.

In the early days of the Republic, the party's membership in Congress—the congressional caucus—chose presidential nominees. Sometimes state and local officials also put forward candidates. National party conventions where delegates were selected by state and local groups began by the 1830s. Each state had different delegate election procedures—some more democratic than others. Custom dictated that the convention sought the candidate. Potential nominees invariably seemed withdrawn and disinterested. They would rarely attend a nominating convention. Any attempt to pursue delegates was considered to be in bad taste. In fact, custom dictated that an official delegation went to the nominee's home to notify him of the party's decision and ask if he would accept. In the early years, convention officials sent a letter. By 1852, the candidate was informed in person. In the 1890s, these notification ceremonies dramatically increased in size. Madison Square Garden in New York City was the site for Grover Cleveland's 1892 notification.

By the first decade of the twentieth century, political reformers considered the convention system most undemocratic. They felt that it was a system dominated by patronage seeking party bosses who ignored the average voter. The primary system began as a way to increase participation in the nominating process. Candidates for the nation's highest office now actually sought the support of convention delegates. Theoretically, the primary allows all party members to choose their party's nominee. Most twentieth century conventions though, have seen a combination of delegates chosen by a political machine and elected in a primary. Today success in the primaries virtually assures the nomination. With few exceptions, the national conventions have become a rubber stamp for the candidate who did the best in the primaries.

The Campaign and Election. The presidential campaign is the great democratic exercise in politics. In recent elections, televised debates between the candidates have become a ritual, attracting record numbers of viewers. Public opinion polls continually monitor the nation's pulse. Commentators and writers analyze campaign strategies. Perhaps the winning strategy is to mobilize the party faithful and to persuade the independent voter that their candidate is the best. This is a costly process and since 1976, the general treasury provides major financial assistance to presidential campaigns. Public funding helps serious presidential candidates to present their qualifications without selling out to wealthy contributors and special interest groups.

Finally, on that first Tuesday after the first Monday in November, the voters make their choice. With the tragic exception of 1860, the American people have accepted the results. (See the article on Abraham Lincoln.) The election process works. Democracy has survived. Forty-one men have held the office of president of the United States. Each has been a powerful personality with varied leadership traits. Each had the opportunity to make major decisions both in foreign and domestic matters which affected the direction of the nation.

Join us as we proceed to study the men who helped to shape our history. We will also learn about their vice presidents, their cabinets, their families, and their homes and monuments.

Fred L. Israel
The City College of the City University of New York

ACKNOWLEDGMENTS

Sir Isaac Newton, the seventeenth-century English scientist who created calculus, discovered that white light is composed of many colors, discovered the law of gravity, and developed the standard laws of motion, once said, "If I have seen farther, it is because I have stood on the shoulders of giants." He meant that he used the work of those who came before him as a starting point for the development of his own ideas. This concept is as true in reference books as it is in science.

The White House Historical Association (740 Jackson Place N.W., Washington, D.C. 20503) supplied all the full page color paintings of the presidents, except seven. They are used with the permission of the White House

Historical Association, and we are grateful to them for their cooperation. The painting of James Monroe is Courtesy of the James Monroe Museum and Memorial Library, Fredericksburg, Virginia; the William Henry Harrison portrait is Courtesy of Grouseland; the John Tyler painting is Courtesy of Sherwood Forest Plantation; the Benjamin Harrison painting is from the President Benjamin Harrison Home; Harry Truman's photograph is from the U.S. Navy, Courtesy Harry S. Truman Library; George Bush's photograph is Courtesy of the Bush Presidential Materials Project; Bill Clinton's photograph is Courtesy of The White House. All the busts of the vice presidents are Courtesy of the Architect of the Capitol.

Over three dozen illustrations are credited to the Collection of David J. and Janice L. Frent. The Frents are friends and neighbors. Fred Israel and I both want to thank them very much for allowing us to show some of the treasures of their unequaled collection of political memorabilia.

The authors of the biographical pieces on the presidents are listed in each volume. They have provided the core of this work, and I am very grateful to them for their cooperation. Dr. Donald A. Ritchie, Associate Historian, United States Senate, wrote all the biographies of the vice presidents. Few people know more about this subject than Dr. Ritchie, and we appreciate his assistance.

Maribeth A. Corona (Editor, Charles E. Smith Books, Inc.) and I have written the sections on Family, Cabinet, and Places. Dr. Israel's editing of our work corrected and improved it greatly although we take full responsibility for any errors that remain. In preparing the material on places, three books served as a starting point: *Presidential Libraries and Museums, An Illustrated Guide,* Pat Hyland (Congressional Quarterly Inc., 1995); *Historic Homes of the American Presidents,* second edition, Irvin Haas (Dover Publications, 1991); and *Cabins, Cottages & Mansions, Homes of the Presidents of the United States,* Nancy D. Myers Benbow and Christopher H. Benbow (Thomas Publications, 1993). We wrote to every place noted in this work and our copy is based on the wealth of information returned to us. It is the most comprehensive and up-to-date collection of information available on this subject.

There is no single book on the families of the presidents. We relied on the abundance of biographies and autobiographies of members of the first families. Also helpful was *Children in the White House,* Christine Sadler (G.P. Putnam's Sons, 1967); *The Presidents' Mothers,* Doris Faber (St. Martin's Press, 1978); and *The First Ladies,* Margaret Brown Klapthor (White House Historical Association, 1989).

The Complete Book of U.S. Presidents, William A. DeGregorio (Wings Books, 1993) is an outstanding one-volume reference work, and we referred to it often. I also had the great pleasure of referring often to three encyclopedias which I had published earlier: *Encyclopedia of the American Presidency,* Leonard W. Levy and Louis Fisher (Simon & Schuster, 1994); *Encyclopedia of the American Constitution,* Leonard W. Levy, Kenneth L. Karst, and Dennis Mahoney (Macmillan & Free Press, 1986); and *Encyclopedia of the United States Congress,* Donald C. Bacon, Roger Davidson, and Morton H. Keller (Simon & Schuster, 1995). I also referred often to *Running for President, The Candidates and Their Images,* Arthur M. Schlesinger, Jr. (Simon & Schuster, 1994). Publishing this two-volume set also gave me the pleasure of working with Professor Schlesinger and the Associate Editors, Fred L. Israel and David J. Frent.

Most of the copyediting was done by Jerilyn Famighetti who was, as usual, prompt, accurate, and pleasant. Our partner in this endeavor was M.E. Aslett Corporation, 95 Campus Plaza, Edison, New Jersey. Although everyone at Aslett lent a hand, special thanks go to Elizabeth Geary, who designed the books; Brian Hewitt and Bob Bovasso, who scanned the images; and Joanne Morbit, who composed the pages. They designed every page and prepared the film for printing. The index was prepared by Jacqueline Flamm.

Charles E. Smith
Freehold, New Jersey

Richard M. Nixon

37TH PRESIDENT

OF THE UNITED STATES OF AMERICA

CHRONOLOGICAL EVENTS

9 January 1913	Born, Yorba Linda, California
9 June 1934	Graduated from Whittier College, California
7 June 1937	Graduated from Duke University Law School, North Carolina and returned to California to practice law
15 June 1942	Commissioned lieutenant, U.S. Navy
5 November 1946	Elected to U.S. House of Representatives
7 November 1950	Elected to U.S. Senate
4 November 1952	Elected vice president
6 November 1956	Reelected vice president
1960	Ran unsuccessfully for president
1962	Ran unsuccessfully for governor of California
5 November 1968	Elected president
20 January 1969	Inaugurated president
February 1972	Traveled to China, opening the way to restored diplomatic relations
May 1972	Traveled to Soviet Union; signed SALT Agreement
17 June 1972	Break-in at Watergate complex
7 November 1972	Reelected president
20 January 1973	Inaugurated president
27 January 1973	Cease-fire reached in Vietnam War
30 January 1973	Watergate burglars convicted
May 1973	Special federal prosecutor appointed to conduct Watergate investigation; U.S. Senate began hearings
10 October 1973	Vice President Spiro Agnew resigned
6 December 1973	Appointed Gerald R. Ford as vice president
27 July 1974	House Judiciary Committee approved three articles of impeachment
9 August 1974	Resigned from the presidency
8 September 1974	Pardoned by President Gerald R. Ford
22 April 1994	Died, New York, New York

BIOGRAPHY

After being soundly defeated in the 1962 gubernatorial race in California, Richard M. Nixon announced he was quitting politics, bitterly asserting, "You won't have Dick Nixon to kick around anymore because, gentlemen, this is my last press conference." His retirement proved short-lived for he soon changed his mind, staged a dramatic comeback, and in 1968 won election as the thirty-seventh president of the United States. One of the most striking things about Nixon's long career was his skill in surviving setbacks, missteps, and disasters. Each time he demonstrated a remarkable persistence and a singular ability to rebuild and reposition himself politically. By the time of his death in 1994, he had even managed to overcome the disgrace of being the only U.S. president to have resigned from that office and was eulogized as a respected elder statesman. An obituary in *Time* magazine concluded: "Other politicians came and went, but Nixon was always coming back. By sheer endurance, he was the most important figure of the postwar era."

EARLY YEARS. Richard Milhous Nixon was born on 9 January 1913 in Yorba Linda, California, not far from Los Angeles. His Quaker parents were hard working but could not make a success of their lemon farm. The family moved in 1922 to Whittier, California, where Nixon attended both high school and college. After earning his law degree at Duke University in 1937, he returned to California and joined Wingert and Bewley, Whittier's oldest law firm. His first case ended in malpractice charges against the firm, but he worked hard and in 1939 became a partner. Meanwhile, ever ambitious, he began laying ground for a political career through active participation in civic affairs. Within the first three years of his return to Whittier, he served as the president of four service organizations. He became, at age 26, the youngest trustee of Whittier College, and began to establish himself in local Republican politics. He also participated in a little theater group in Whittier. It was there in 1938 that he met Thelma Catherine "Pat" Ryan, a business education teacher at Whittier High School. After dating for over two years, they were married on 21 June 1940.

U.S. REPRESENTATIVE. The couple moved to Washington, D.C. in 1942. Nixon worked briefly for the Office of Price Administration before joining the U.S. Navy later that year. During the remainder of the war, he served in the South Pacific Combat Transport Command. In the fall of 1945, a group of small businessmen and ranchers from southern California approached Nixon about running as the Republican candidate for his home district's seat in the U.S. House of Representatives. He jumped at the chance and returned to Whittier after his discharge from the navy in early 1946. With his wife as his only full-time staff, they used their savings for both personal expenses and the campaign. Nixon hit the campaign trail in February, just before Pat gave birth to their first daughter, Patricia (Tricia). Taking advantage of postwar fears, he used "Red Scare" tactics, accusing the Democratic incumbent of being a communist sympathizer supported by organized labor and its communist infiltrators. While his charges were untrue, the voters believed him. Nixon won, establishing his reputation as a ruthless street fighter determined to win whatever the costs.

Nixon used the same issue to grab national attention when he took his seat in the U.S. House of Representatives. He managed to secure a position on the House Committee on Un-American Activities (HUAC), which was charged with rooting out communists in government. In the fall of 1948, when he was in the middle of his reelection campaign (and shortly after the birth of his second daughter, Julie), Nixon took the lead in the Committee's investigation of accusations made by Whittaker Chambers. Chambers was an admitted former Communist Party member, who claimed that communists had infiltrated the government. One of the individuals named by Chambers was Alger Hiss, an official in the State Department from 1936 through 1947. Nixon, convinced that Hiss was guilty, pursued leads over the following months, expanding the charges from perjury before the committee to espionage and treason. Ultimately, Hiss was convicted only of perjury (the statute of limitations had run out on the espionage charges), but that conviction justified Nixon's actions. The name of Alger Hiss became synonymous with communist subversion. Nixon, as the man who had exposed him, won national recognition from a public caught up in the extreme fear of the cold war.

Capitalizing on the publicity of the Hiss case, Nixon in 1950 won the Republican nomination for one of California's seats in the U.S. Senate. He then launched a full-scale attack against his Democratic opponent, Helen Gahagan Douglas, a New Deal liberal who had served in the House since 1945. Using the same tactics he had employed in 1946, Nixon accused Douglas of being "soft on Communism," calling her the "Pink Lady." Douglas, for her part, responded to Nixon's ruthless and aggressive campaign tactics by calling him "Tricky Dick," a nickname that stuck with him throughout his political career. Once again his "Red Scare" tactics paid off—he won the November election by nearly 700,000 votes.

VICE PRESIDENT. Nixon's Senate career proved short-lived. In mid-1952, Dwight D. Eisenhower chose him to be his running mate on the Republican presidential ticket. Shortly after the campaign began, however, his place on the ticket was threatened by the disclosure of a special fund of $18,000 set up for him by a group of California supporters. Concerned about the appropriateness of such a gift and the possible paybacks and special favors that might have been expected, some of Eisenhower's advisers urged that Nixon resign from the ticket. In one of his classic political comebacks, Nixon took the issue to the American

people in a live television address on 23 September 1952. In an emotional and dramatic performance, he successfully defended himself and took on his accusers. He insisted that the money had been used to pay for office costs only and not personal expenses. The speech became known as the "Checkers Speech," in reference to his daughters' cocker spaniel, the only gift he claimed he or his family had received. Nixon stayed on the ticket, and the Republicans regained the White House after a 20-year absence. In just six years, Richard Nixon had risen from small-town lawyer to vice president of the United States.

President Eisenhower had little interest in partisan politics, leaving the way open for Nixon to assume the role of party leader and develop the political connections critical to his next goal—the 1960 Republican presidential nomination. By the time the party's convention opened in July 1960, the nomination was his. On the campaign trail, he tried to emphasize the importance of continuing the progress of the Eisenhower years, but the key factor turned out to be an unprecedented face-to-face television debate between Nixon and John F. Kennedy, the Democratic candidate. Political observers claimed that Nixon lost the election in that debate. He appeared tired, sweating, and ill at ease compared to the calm, cool, and photogenic

President Eisenhower did not give Nixon many responsibilities. However, Nixon did make many trips abroad. On 10 December 1953, Vice President and Mrs. Nixon met with the President of Burma and his niece. (Courtesy National Archives.)

The State Department asked Vice President Nixon to represent the United States at the inauguration of Arturo Frondizi as president of Argentina. This became a trip of more than two weeks throughout South America. The trip ended in Caracas, Venezuela, where an angry mob almost killed Nixon and his wife. Perez Jimenez, who had been the despised dictator of Venezuela for 10 years, had fled to exile in the United States. Communist and nationalist groups in Venezuela were very angry with the United States for allowing this. A bloodthirsty mob took out their anger on the Nixons. They stoned their car and almost tipped it over.

Nixon described their homecoming (15 May 1958) in his first book, Six Crises: "Fifteen thousand people greeted us when we arrived at the National Airport the next morning. President Eisenhower put protocol aside to meet Mrs. Nixon and me at the airport. He was accompanied by the entire Cabinet. The Democratic as well as the Republican leadership of Congress was there. Several large groups of Latin American students studying in the Washington area were also on hand. . . ." (Courtesy Dwight D. Eisenhower Library.)

Kennedy. Kennedy won the election by only 120,000 popular votes but secured a clear majority of 303 votes in the Electoral College.

ELECTION AS PRESIDENT. Defeated, Nixon returned to California and practiced law briefly before returning to politics in the disastrous 1962 California gubernatorial campaign that led to his famous "last press conference." But it was not long before he began to rethink his retirement from politics. In what observers hailed as one of history's most remarkable political comebacks, Nixon secured the 1968 Republican presidential nomination. He chose as his running mate a relative unknown, Spiro T. Agnew, then governor of Maryland. Running against Hubert H. Humphrey, the Democratic candidate, and George Wallace, the American Independent Party candidate, Nixon drew on popular resentments against the disruptions of the 1960s—civil rights protests and urban violence, opposition to the Vietnam war, the

counterculture, women's liberation, and the sexual revolution. He called on the "silent majority" of the middle class to cast their votes for the traditional values and morality of the Republican Party. Although the popular vote was close, Nixon carried 32 states. He became the nation's thirty-seventh president—the twelfth former vice president to be elected president but the first who did not succeed the president under whom he served.

During the time he was vice president, Nixon had been troubled by the lack of order and organization within the executive branch. He was determined to take control of the situation as president. Looking to corporate models rather than cabinet government, Nixon and his advisers centralized power within the Oval Office through a variety of administrative and legislative actions. Like his predecessors, John F. Kennedy and Lyndon B. Johnson, he asserted the centrality of the presidency to the national agenda. Convinced

Question. How would you label yourself?

Nixon. Labels mean different things to different people. The nineteenth-century liberal is the twentieth-century conservative and the nineteenth-century conservative (with a small c) is the twentieth-century liberal. For example, in the conservative-liberal dialogue, which began in eighteenth-century America, probably the major difference was that the conservatives then were for strong central government. Hamilton was a strong central government man, whereas the liberals like Jefferson were for individual liberties, for decentralization of power.

In the twentieth century the liberals became the strong central government people—all power should be consolidated in Washington—and the conservatives became the people who were for decentralization.

Well, basically I'm a strong advocate of individual liberties. I'm very skeptical about centralized power. I believe in strong local government.

Now let's take this conservative-liberal dialogue as it relates to foreign policy. The conservatives have been considered the isolationists and the internationalists were considered to be the liberals. So looking at my record you would have to say I'm a liberal on foreign policy. Because I recognize America's role in the world I am not an isolationist. I have supported foreign aid, for instance.

But the old liberals who were internationalists 20 years ago now are turning inward. They are telling us to get out of Asia and Latin America, that we're overcommitted. My view, however, hasn't changed. While I make it very clear that we have to get other nations to assume their share of the responsibility, I also believe that we cannot withdraw from the world. Am I a conservative or a liberal? My answer is that I'm an internationalist.

- *Richard M. Nixon's statements describing his political philosophy. 5 May 1968.*

that cabinet meetings were inefficient if not counterproductive, Nixon shifted the focus of policy-making from the cabinet to loyalists within the White House staff. This "imperial" approach to the presidency was also behind a series of structural changes he instituted in the executive branch, especially the establishment of the Office of Management and Budget. He took the old Bureau of the Budget and remade it into a powerful monitoring and investigatory unit under his control. This restructuring created Nixon's own personal bureaucracy despite Nixon's long-standing dislike of bureaucracy. The executive office grew from 4 agencies and 570 employees in 1969 to 20 agencies and over 6,000 employees in 1972.

Nixon was also determined to reassert the power of the president in comparison to Congress. When congressional committees called aides to testify on administration policies or activities, Nixon blocked them, claiming executive privilege (the confidentiality of private presidential communication) or the preservation of national security. When Congress took action he opposed, he used his veto power. When that did not work, he seized and set aside funds. Of course, whenever possible, he simply took action unilaterally, briefing Congress after the fact.

FOREIGN POLICY. Nowhere was Nixon's concept of the modern presidency more clear than in his handling of international issues. He shifted foreign policy decision-making from the State Department to the White House and the National Security Council and undertook major new initiatives without consulting Congress. This was particularly the case in regard to the war in Vietnam. The involvement of the United States in Vietnam, begun under

Truman and Eisenhower, had grown to massive proportions under Kennedy and Johnson. Nixon recognized that this involvement had to end but promised in the 1968 campaign to achieve "peace with honor." Rather than wait for stalled peace talks to bear fruit, he announced in March 1969 a plan to shift responsibility for combat to South Vietnamese troops—called "Vietnamization"—and to begin withdrawing U.S. troops. He later broadened this policy into the Nixon Doctrine limiting U.S. military involvement abroad. But at the same time, he secretly pursued two other strategies—expansion of the war into Laos and Cambodia and secret negotiations with the North Vietnamese.

Although he authorized secret bombing of communist areas and supply depots in Cambodia in March 1969, the public did not learn of U.S. involvement there until a year later. Protests followed on college campuses. The most notable was a demonstration at Kent State University in May 1970 that left four students dead and nine wounded. Despite this growing opposition to escalation of the war, Nixon continued with his secret strategy, providing air, artillery, and logistical (the procurement, distribution, maintenance, and replacement of material and personnel) support for a South Vietnamese invasion of Laos in February 1971.

Meanwhile, Henry Kissinger, Nixon's special assistant for national security, carried on secret negotiations with the North Vietnamese. Little progress was made in the peace talks, however, until Nixon, in response to threats of a North Vietnamese offensive, ordered the mining of North Vietnamese ports and increased bombing of Hanoi, the capital of North Vietnam. North Vietnam then agreed to a new series of meetings with Kissinger, leading up to Kissinger's announcement on 26 October, conveniently just before the 1972 election, that peace was "at hand." The agreement fell apart shortly thereafter, however, and on 18 December 1972 Nixon ordered the bombing of North Vietnam to resume. North Vietnam then agreed to continue negotiations,

and on 27 January a cease-fire agreement was reached. Nixon's determination to "win the peace" prolonged the war for four more years. This cost thousands of lives and ended up with terms not substantially different from a North Vietnamese proposal in 1969. Significantly, the Paris Peace Accords did not constitute a treaty and thus were not submitted to the Senate for approval. Congress, however, took action of its own. In November 1973, Congress overrode Nixon's veto of a war powers act that required congressional approval of any presidential commitment of U.S. combat troops abroad.

Nixon's decision to seek "peace with honor" rather than simply withdraw from Vietnam won him significant support from conservative cold war warriors and gave him the ability to improve relations with the People's Republic of China and the Soviet Union. Taking advantage of a growing split between the two communist powers, Nixon began raising the possibility of rapprochement (establishing friendly relations) with China early in 1969, but it was not until 1971 that the Chinese indicated real interest. The United States then ended restrictions on U.S. travel to China. This opened the way for a highly publicized Ping-Pong match between Chinese and U.S. teams, a secret trip to China by Kissinger that spring, and a public trip the following October. Then, as trade reopened between the two nations, Nixon himself made a historic trip to China in February 1972. This led to the exchange of unofficial delegations the following year. The normalization of relations with China was a considerable accomplishment for Nixon. This was ironic, given his earlier condemnation of the Democrats for "selling out" China in 1949 and failing to stop the Communist Chinese in Korea.

After the United States established relations with China, the Soviet Union was more open to Nixon's efforts at détente (the easing of tensions). This strategy bypassed traditional diplomatic channels and demonstrated again the White House's control over foreign policy. Negotiations between the two powers led to a series of formal summit agreements signed by Nixon and Leonid I. Brezhnev during Nixon's visit to the Soviet Union in May 1972. Ultimately, while Nixon's détente strategy improved U. S.–Soviet relations for a time, it did not prove a successful vehicle for disarmament, failing to produce a treaty limiting offensive weapons.

DOMESTIC POLICY. The Nixon Doctrine was a practical effort to break with his predecessors' preoccupation with containing or preventing Soviet expansion and reassess responsibility in international affairs. His New Federalism was an attempt to move beyond the New Deal and the Great Society and recast the role of the federal government in relation to state and local governments on domestic issues. His goal was not to cut back on federal spending for social programs but to establish national goals and disperse responsibility and the funds for such programs through revenue sharing and other vehicles. The New Federalism was most clearly spelled out in the Family Assistance Program, a welfare reform proposal by the Nixon administration in 1969 that would have shifted the federal government's role from providing services such as Medicaid, food stamps, and school lunches to providing income through direct cash payments to the poor, essentially a guaranteed annual income for all heads of poor households.

When liberal critics found the proposed minimum income much too low and conservatives opposed the whole idea of a guaranteed income, the proposal was doomed and died in the Senate. While Nixon could not claim success in welfare reform, he could point to achievements in related areas, such as increased funding for students from low income families and cost-of-living adjustments for Social Security recipients.

On the negative side, his efforts to dismantle the Office of Economic Opportunity, established by Lyndon Johnson to aid the poor, were seen as an attack on advocacy programs for the poor, despite the administration's claim that the goal was simply to eliminate waste and inefficiency. Regardless of the success or failure of specific programs or policies, expenditures for social welfare services under Nixon increased from $55 billion in 1970 to $132 billion in 1975. As a percentage of the federal budget, social welfare expenditures increased from 28 percent in 1970 to 40.4 percent in 1975, with such expenditures exceeding defense spending for the first time since World War II.

The Nixon administration's record on civil rights, however, provoked more debate and criticism. Throughout the 1960s African Americans were growing increasingly frustrated by the lack of progress in civil rights and school desegregation. That frustration in turn led to protests and violence. Nixon was opposed to forced remedies such as busing. In the 1968 campaign he promised to slow down school desegregation. Even after the Supreme Court ordered that desegregation should proceed "at once" and mandated busing, Nixon remained firmly opposed. In 1972 he even proposed a legislative suspension on busing. Moreover, he objected to using federal funding as a bargaining tool with noncompliant school districts. He shifted enforcement to the Justice Department, where time-consuming litigation would slow the pace. Nevertheless, substantial progress was actually made in school desegregation during the Nixon years. In 1968, 68 percent of African American children in the South attended black schools, and 40 percent of African American children nationally attended segregated schools. By 1972, that had dropped to 8 percent and 12 percent respectively. Other achievements in the area of civil rights during the Nixon years included the strengthening of the Equal Employment Opportunity Commission, establishing the Office of Minority Business Enterprise, and shifting federal policy in regard to Native Americans from an integrationist approach to recognition of tribal autonomy and land claims.

Nixon wanted to establish a conservative majority on the Supreme Court. This was tied to Nixon's opposition to the Supreme Court's desegregation decisions. It was consistent with both his concerns about the Court as a policy maker and his hopes to attract white Southern voters. Four positions on the Supreme Court came open during his tenure.

(Left to right) John N. Mitchell, President Nixon, J. Edgar Hoover, and John D. Ehrlichman met in May 1971. Attorney General Mitchell resigned in 1972 to become director of the Committee to Reelect the President. He went to prison for 19 months for perjury and other crimes in connection with Watergate.

Hoover was director of the FBI from 1924 until his death in 1972. Nixon did not trust Hoover. In Years of Upheaval, *Secretary of State Henry Kissinger said that Nixon believed that Hoover was capable of blackmailing him and he "was determined to get rid of Hoover at the earliest opportunity after the 1972 election. . . ."*

Ehrlichman was one of Nixon's closest aides. He resigned on 30 April 1973. On 22 May Nixon said that Ehrlichman had been involved in a White House cover-up without his knowledge. Ehrlichman was later convicted for his involvement in Watergate. (Courtesy National Archives.)

Although the Senate rejected two of his nominees (both Southerners), he won confirmation of Warren E. Burger as chief justice in 1969. Harry Blackmun, Lewis Powell, and William H. Rehnquist were also confirmed. Each was viewed as a strict constructionist, committed to a more restricted interpretation of the Constitution and a more limited role for the Court. Nevertheless, the Burger Court did not retreat into a more passive role. In several cases it actually expanded rights, most notably in 1973 in *Roe v. Wade.* This landmark decision upholding a woman's right to abortion was written by Blackmun, a Nixon appointee.

Nixon tried a variety of measures to address the problems of the economy but never achieved more than temporary success. At first, he tried to use traditional monetary and fiscal tools to slow inflation yet keep the economy growing. Finally,

despite his commitment to free-market principles, Nixon became convinced in 1971 that wage and price controls were necessary to curb inflation. His New Economic Policy announced that year included such controls and devalued the dollar to address the decline in gold reserves and the trade deficit. These measures slowed the pace of inflation for a time. In 1972, when he was up for reelection, he could claim responsibility for an economic upturn. It was the first such election-year achievement since the end of World War II. But by 1973, inflation was growing again. In Nixon's last year in office, fuel shortages brought on by an oil embargo and higher prices by Middle Eastern producers weakened the U.S. economy and led to recession once again.

WATERGATE. Although Nixon won reelection in 1972 in a landslide over the Democratic challenger, George McGovern, he was unable to give either foreign policy or domestic issues his full attention in the months that followed as he and his staff tried to deal with the Watergate investigation. The investigation began with two break-ins at the Democratic National Committee offices in Washington's Watergate complex in spring 1972. The White House denied any involvement despite the indictment in September of two former White House aides and a staff member of the Committee for the Reelection of the President (CRP also referred to as CREEP). Over the course of the winter of 1972–1973, the full story began to emerge, not only linking the CRP directly to the burglaries but also indicating that White House officials had tried to obstruct the investigation and hide White House involvement. On 30 April, insisting that he knew nothing of the burglaries or any attempt to obstruct the investigation, Nixon accepted the resignations of three top aides implicated in the cover-up. But the investigation did not end there. In May 1973, at the prodding of Congress, Attorney General Elliot L. Richardson appointed a special federal prosecutor to take charge of the Watergate investigation. That same month the Senate Select Committee on Presidential Campaign Activities began nationally televised hearings that included testimony by a former Nixon aide that the President had been aware of the cover-up at least as early as September 1972. The most startling revelation from the hearings, however, was that since 1971 all Oval Office conversations had been tape recorded. Both the special prosecutor, Archibald Cox, and the Senate committee subpoenaed the tapes, but Nixon refused to release them, citing executive privilege. Then on 20 October 1973, in what was called the "Saturday Night Massacre," both Attorney General Richardson and Deputy Attorney General William D. Ruckelshaus, resigned rather than carry out Nixon's order to fire Cox. Bipartisan calls for impeachment followed.

By that point, the tide was beginning to shift against Nixon. The Watergate investigation had uncovered details not only about the break-ins

and the attempted cover-up but also about the White House Special Investigative Unit (known as the "plumbers" because their job was to stop leaks), the Nixon's "enemies list," and the various wiretaps, break-ins, dirty tricks, and other forms of harassment directed by the President's staff since 1969. Moreover, Watergate was only one of a number of investigations into charges against Nixon and his associates. Other charges included whether government funds had been used improperly to improve Nixon's San Clemente, California home; whether Nixon had claimed improper income tax deductions; and whether Vice President Agnew had taken kickbacks as governor of Maryland and as vice president. The last charge ended with Agnew's resignation on 10 October 1973, after pleading *nolo contendere* (no contest) in response to a grand jury indictment for graft. Nixon subsequently appointed Gerald R. Ford, congressman from Michigan and leader of the House Republicans, as vice president. This was the first such appointment under procedures established by the Twenty-fifth Amendment (ratified in 1967).

On 22 October, just two days after the "Saturday Night Massacre," the House of Representatives

---

Amendment XXV

SECTION 2. Whenever there is a vacancy in the office of the office of the Vice President, the President shall nominate a Vice President who shall take office upon confirmation by a majority of both Houses of Congress.

- *For the complete text of the Constitution of the United States, see Volume 8.*

---

directed its Judiciary Committee to begin investigation into possible grounds for impeachment of the president. The next day Nixon agreed to turn over the subpoenaed tapes to a federal court only to report later that two of the tapes had never existed and a portion of a third had been mysteriously erased. This further fueled the demands for a full investigation, and Nixon was forced to appoint a new Watergate special prosecutor, who in March 1974 brought indictments against key White House and CRP staff for participation in the Watergate cover-up. When the special prosecutor subpoenaed additional tapes, Nixon again refused to comply. In July 1974, the Supreme Court ruled unanimously that he must surrender the tapes.

The House Judiciary Committee held televised hearings that summer, climaxing in a vote on 27 July 1974, to introduce in the House three articles of impeachment (obstruction of justice, abuse of presidential power, and refusal to obey House subpoenas). Then on 5 August, Nixon released tapes that included a conversation on 23 June 1972 (six days after the second burglary), in which the President ordered an effort to halt the FBI's investigation of the Watergate break-in—clear evidence that Nixon had participated in the cover-up and had lied about what he knew.

Impeachment in the House and conviction in the Senate was now almost a certainty. Nixon announced on 8 August that he would resign from the presidency and on 9 August became the first U.S. president to resign from office. While Nixon never stood trial for his role in Watergate—on 8 September 1974, President Ford granted him an unconditional pardon—more than 30 men he worked with went to jail.

After his resignation, Nixon retreated for a time but then returned once again, reinstated as an elder statesman. In retirement, he wrote nine books (and a tenth was in page proof at his death), including *RN: The Memoirs of Richard Nixon*. He also traveled the world (including return trips to China and the Soviet Union) and advised each of his successors, both Republicans and Democrats. He died of a stroke on 22 April 1994 in New York. In testimony to his rehabilitation, President Bill Clinton and all four former presidents (Ford, Carter, Reagan, and Bush) attended his funeral on 27 April at the Richard Nixon Library in his home town of Yorba Linda, California.

With his daughter, Tricia, at his side, Nixon resigned from office on 9 August 1974.
(Courtesy National Archives.)

▲   *One indication of Nixon's rehabilitation is the fact that the dedication of the Richard Nixon Library & Birthplace in Yorba Linda on 19 July 1990 was attended by President and Mrs. Bush and former Presidents Ford and Reagan and their wives.* (Courtesy The Richard Nixon Library & Birthplace.)

(Courtesy The Richard Nixon Library & Birthplace.)

◀   *"Most men mature around a central core; Nixon had several. This is why he was never at peace with himself. Any attempt to sum up his complex character in one attribute is bound to be misleading. The detractors' view that Nixon was the incarnation of evil is as wrong as the adulation of his more fervent admirers. On closer acquaintance one realized that what gave Nixon his driven quality was the titanic struggle among the various personalities within him. And it was a struggle that never ended; there was never a permanent victor between the dark and the sensitive sides of his nature. Now one, now another personality predominated, creating an overall impression of menace, of torment, of unpredictability, and, in the final analysis, of enormous vulnerability."* Henry Kissinger, Years of Upheaval.

VICE PRESIDENT

Spiro Theodore Agnew
(1918–1996)

CHRONOLOGICAL EVENTS

1918	Born, Baltimore, Maryland, 9 November
1941	Enlisted in the U.S. Army
1947	Graduated from University of Baltimore Law School
1962	Elected Baltimore County executive
1966	Elected governor of Maryland
1968	Elected vice president
1973	Resigned as vice president
1996	Died, Ocean City, Maryland, 17 September

BIOGRAPHY

The only vice president to resign because of criminal charges, Spiro Theodore Agnew was born in Baltimore, Maryland. He worked at a grocery store and insurance agency to pay his way through college. During World War II, he won a Bronze Star. After the war, the G.I. Bill of Rights paid for his law degree.

Moving to the Baltimore suburbs to practice law, Agnew registered as a Republican. In 1962, he was elected Baltimore County executive. In 1966, he ran for governor against a Democrat who favored housing segregation. Democratic liberals broke ranks to help Agnew win.

Riots in Baltimore after the assassination of Martin Luther King Jr. in 1968 caused Governor Agnew to condemn African American leaders for not standing up to the rioters. That event encouraged Richard M. Nixon, the Republican presidential nominee, to select Agnew as his running mate in order to appeal to voters angry over urban rioting. Agnew was so unknown that the press asked "Spiro who?"

Nixon made Agnew the first vice president to have an office in the West Wing of the White House. Agnew planned to lobby for the administration on Capitol Hill, but Republican senators resented his arm-twisting. He got a similarly cool response from the White House staff. Instead, the administration dispatched Agnew to deliver speeches attacking Nixon's opponents. He criticized the network news media for their liberal bias and branded other critics "impudent snobs" and "nattering nabobs of negativism." Agnew's hostile speeches so boosted his popularity that they alarmed Nixon.

In 1972, Nixon sought to replace Agnew on the ticket with Treasury Secretary John Connally. But Connally considered the vice presidency "useless" and declined. Agnew won reelection and started planning to succeed Nixon in 1976. As President Nixon grew entangled in the Watergate scandal, Vice President Agnew learned that he was being investigated in Maryland for bribery and income tax evasion. In September 1973, a combative Agnew told his supporters, "I will not resign if indicted!"

White House chief of staff Alexander Haig worried that the impeachment of both the president and the vice president would make the Democratic Speaker of the House president. Haig informed Agnew that unless he resigned and pleaded guilty, he would go to jail. On 10 October 1973, Agnew resigned and pleaded *nolo contendere* (no contest) to income tax evasion. He died on 17 September 1996 in Ocean City, Maryland.

VICE PRESIDENT

Gerald Rudolph Ford
(1913–)

CHRONOLOGICAL EVENTS

1913	Born, Omaha, Nebraska, 14 July
1935	Graduated from University of Michigan
1941	Graduated from Yale Law School, Connecticut
1942	Enlisted in the U.S. Navy
1948	Elected to U.S. House of Representatives
1965	Elected House minority leader
1973	Appointed vice president
1974	Became president upon the resignation of Richard M. Nixon
1976	Ran unsuccessfully for president

BIOGRAPHY

Gerald R. Ford served as the United States's first nonelected vice president and president. He was born Leslie Lynch King and renamed for his adopted father. Ford grew up in Grand Rapids, Michigan and attended the University of Michigan. A star football player in college, he received offers to play professional football but instead went to Yale Law School. During World War II, he served in the navy in the Pacific.

An internationalist, Ford defeated an isolationist incumbent for the Republican nomination to a seat in the U.S. House of Representatives in 1948. Regularly reelected afterward, he began his climb through the House leadership. In 1963, President Lyndon Johnson appointed Ford to the Warren Commission, which investigated the assassination of John F. Kennedy. Also that year, Ford was elected chairman of the House Republican Conference. In 1965, a group of "Young Turk" Republicans made Ford their candidate against the incumbent Republican minority leader, Charles Halleck. As House minority leader, Ford led the opposition to President Johnson's "Great Society" legislation. An irritated Johnson grumbled that Ford could not "walk and chew gum at the same time."

Ford campaigned diligently for Republican congressional candidates across the country and also supported Richard M. Nixon for president. Mentioned as a potential vice presidential candidate with Nixon in 1968, Ford preferred to remain in the House and become Speaker. Although House Republicans remained in the minority throughout Nixon's administration, Ford loyally promoted the President's legislative agenda. When Vice President Spiro Agnew resigned in 1973, the Twenty-fifth Amendment permitted President Nixon to nominate a replacement. Nixon considered a list of candidates, and most congressional leaders recommended Ford as the next vice president.

Confirmed by the U.S. Senate, Ford took the oath as vice president in the House chamber. In an effort to reassure the public, he spent most of his eight months as vice president traveling throughout the country giving speeches. Ford stood behind the President faithfully during the Watergate investigation and refused to discuss Nixon's impeachment or resignation from office.

On 9 August 1974, Richard M. Nixon resigned as president. Ford was sworn in to succeed him, proclaiming that "our long national nightmare is over."

THE CABINET

SECRETARY OF STATE
William P. Rogers, 1969
Henry A. Kissinger, 1973

SECRETARY OF THE TREASURY
David M. Kennedy, 1969
John B. Connally, Jr., 1971
George P. Shultz, 1972
William E. Simon, 1974

POSTMASTER GENERAL[1]
Wilton M. Blount, 1969

ATTORNEY GENERAL
John N. Mitchell, 1969
Richard G. Kleindienst, 1972
Elliot L. Richardson, 1973
William B. Saxbe, 1974

SECRETARY OF THE INTERIOR
Walter J. Hickel, 1969
Rogers C.B. Morton, 1971

SECRETARY OF AGRICULTURE
Clifford M. Hardin, 1969
Earl L. Butz, 1971

SECRETARY OF COMMERCE
Maurice H. Stans, 1969
Peter G. Peterson, 1972
Frederick B. Dent, 1973

SECRETARY OF LABOR
George P. Shultz, 1969
James D. Hodgson, 1970
Peter J. Brennan, 1973

1. On 1 July 1971, the Post Office Department became the semi-independent U.S. Postal Service with non-cabinet status.

Caspar Weinburger is shown here with President Nixon in the Oval Office. (Courtesy Nixon Materials Staff, National Archives.)

Caspar W. Weinburger (1917–). Weinburger was appointed secretary of health, education, and welfare by President Richard M. Nixon in 1973. He had previously served as budget director.

As secretary of health, education, and welfare, Weinburger served on the President's Cancer Advisory Panel, which proposed an intense research program to find a cure for the disease. After President Nixon's resignation, he retained his post in the administration of Gerald R. Ford, resigning in 1975.

In 1981, he was appointed secretary of defense by President Ronald Reagan. Weinburger directed the largest military buildup in U.S. peacetime history. He also supported the Strategic Defense Initiative defense system, also known as "Star Wars."

THE CABINET

SECRETARY OF DEFENSE
Melvin R. Laird, 1969
Elliot L. Richardson, 1973
James R. Schlesinger, 1973

SECRETARY OF HEALTH, EDUCATION, AND WELFARE
Robert H. Finch, 1969
Elliot L. Richardson, 1970
Caspar W. Weinburger, 1973

SECRETARY OF HOUSING AND URBAN DEVELOPMENT
George W. Romney, 1969
James T. Lynn, 1973

SECRETARY OF TRANSPORTATION
John A. Volpe, 1969
Claude S. Brinegar, 1973

John N. Mitchell (1913–1988). Mitchell was appointed attorney general by President Richard M. Nixon in 1969.

As attorney general, Mitchell approved the prosecution of the "Chicago Seven" for their involvement in the disruption at the 1968 Democratic Convention. He opposed busing to achieve a racial balance in state school systems. He also increased federal efforts to stop drug trafficking.

In March 1972, Mitchell resigned to become head of the Committee to Reelect the President (CRP). In 1974, he was indicted by a federal grand jury for his involvement in the Watergate break-ins. On 1 January 1975, Mitchell was found guilty of conspiracy, obstruction of justice, and perjury. He served 19 months in prison.

John N. Mitchell (left) is shown here with President Richard M. Nixon at the U.S. Attorneys Conference on 11 June 1970. (Courtesy Nixon Materials Staff, National Archives.)

FAMILY

CHRONOLOGICAL EVENTS

16 March 1912	Thelma Catherine (Pat) Ryan born	5 July 1948	Daughter, Julie, born
21 June 1940	Pat Ryan married Richard M. Nixon	22 June 1993	Pat Nixon died
		22 April 1994	Richard M. Nixon died
21 February 1946	Daughter, Patricia (Tricia), born		

(Courtesy The Richard Nixon Library & Birthplace.)

Pat Ryan was a teenager when both of her parents died. She put herself through college and graduated with honors from the University of Southern California. She met Richard M. Nixon through a local theater group, and he proposed to her on the day they met. She suffered strokes in 1976 and 1983 and died in 1993 at her home in Park Ridge, New Jersey.

In *Pat Nixon: The Untold Story,* Julie Nixon Eisenhower writes: "During their courtship, my father was drawn to the wistful quality in young Patricia Ryan, this woman of dreams of whom he wrote in 1939, 'You have the finest ideals of anyone I have ever known.' He was drawn also to 'the vagabond within you that makes you want to go far places and see great things.' Together they traveled far, but by a turn of fate, most of their journey was taken in the public eye. Although my mother continued to believe intensely in the causes that kept the Nixons in public life, the political road was not easy for one who had always valued her privacy and independence. At the center of an ever-widening life involving world travel and leaders, campaigns and political controversies, she continued to have her feet firmly planted on the ground."

The Nixons flew to California in June 1959. Tricia, age 14, is next to her father. Julie, age 12, is holding her mother's hand. (Courtesy National Archives.) ▶

Tricia Nixon (left) graduated from Finch College. She married Edward Cox in a White House ceremony in 1971. Julie graduated from Smith College. She married David Eisenhower, the President's grandson, in 1968. She wrote a biography of her mother, Pat Nixon: The Untold Story. *(Courtesy The Richard Nixon Library & Birthplace.)* ▼

THE RICHARD NIXON LIBRARY & BIRTHPLACE

18001 Yorba Linda Boulevard • Yorba Linda, California 92686 • Tel: (714) 993-3393

Located off Highway 57, about 45 minutes from Los Angeles International Airport. Open Monday to Saturday from 10 A.M. to 5 P.M.; Sundays from 11 A.M. to 5 P.M. Closed Thanksgiving, Christmas, and New Year's Day. Admission fee, with discounts available for groups of 20 or more. Children ages 7 and under admitted free. Handicapped accessible. Gift shop and bookstore. Special events include an annual celebration of President Nixon's birthday on 9 January and a White House Christmas Program in December. It is the first presidential museum to be built and operated entirely without taxpayers' funds.

At the dedication ceremony of the library on 19 July 1990, Richard Nixon stated: "What you will see here, among other things, is a personal life—the influence of a strong family, of inspirational ministers, of great teachers. You will see a political life—running for Congress, running for the Senate, running for governor, running for president three times. And you will see the life of a great nation—77 years of it. A period in which we had unprecedented progress for the United States. And you will see great leaders—leaders who changed the world, who helped to make the world what we have today." (Courtesy The Richard Nixon Library & Birthplace.)

The Nixon Library & Birthplace covers nine of the original twelve-acre citrus grove that belonged to Nixon's parents, Frank and Hannah. The site contains a 52,000-square-foot main gallery and archives, a 293-seat motion-picture theater, a 75-seat amphitheater, a 3,000-square-foot reflecting pool, the First Lady's Garden, and the original birthplace home. On 19 July 1990, the site was dedicated by President Bush and former Presidents Nixon, Ford, and Reagan.

Included in the self-guided tour of the birthplace home is an audio program, narrated by President Nixon, in which he tells the story of his childhood years in Yorba Linda, California: "As a young boy in Yorba Linda, I never thought of becoming President of the United States, or even entering politics. My goal was to become a railroad engineer. Sometimes at night I was awakened by the sound of a train whistle, and I would dream of the far-off places I wanted to visit someday." (Courtesy The Richard Nixon Library & Birthplace.)

In 1911, Richard Nixon's parents, Frank and Hannah, purchased 12 acres of land in Yorba Linda, California. Nixon's father built a one-and-a-half-story, five-room house on the property, and in 1913, Richard Nixon was born in his parents' bedroom on the first floor. He spent his childhood in Yorba Linda until his family moved to nearby Whittier in 1922, when he was nine years old.

The birthplace home is part of the Richard Nixon Library & Birthplace. It has been restored to its appearance during Nixon's childhood and contains original furnishings, including the bed in which he was born and the piano which he played as a child.

An audio program, narrated by Nixon, describes the home, its furnishings, and his childhood memories there. The second floor is not open to the public.

Gerald R. Ford

38TH PRESIDENT
OF THE UNITED STATES OF AMERICA

CHRONOLOGICAL EVENTS

14 July 1913	Born Leslie Lynch King Jr., Omaha, Nebraska
17 June 1935	Graduated from University of Michigan
18 June 1941	Graduated from Yale Law School, New Haven, Connecticut
7 June 1941	Admitted to bar, Grand Rapids, Michigan
1942–1946	Served in U.S. Navy
2 November 1948	Elected to U.S. House of Representatives
4 January 1965	Elected House minority leader
6 December 1973	Sworn in as vice president
9 August 1974	Became president upon Richard M. Nixon's resignation
8 September 1974	Pardoned former President Nixon
16 September 1974	Announced amnesty program for draft evaders and deserters
20 August 1974	Nominated Nelson A. Rockefeller for vice president
8 October 1974	Announced "Whip Inflation Now" campaign
23 April 1975	Ordered evacuation of Saigon
1 August 1975	Signed Helsinki Agreement
5 September 1975	Assassination attempt
22 September 1975	Second assassination attempt
14 May 1975	Ordered military operation to rescue the crewmen of the *Mayaguez* from Cambodian captors
2 November 1976	Defeated for reelection as president
20 January 1977	Retired to Rancho Mirage, California
1979	Published memoirs, *A Time to Heal*

BIOGRAPHY

Gerald R. Ford's goal was to be Speaker of the U.S. House of Representatives. In 1972, when the Republicans failed to gain control of the House, despite President Richard M. Nixon's landslide reelection victory, Ford decided that his goal could not be reached. He told friends and family then that he would retire from Congress in 1977. His political career did come to an end that year, but the office he left was the U.S. presidency, an office he held for only 30 months as a result of a unique set of circumstances. Upon the resignation of Vice President Spiro T. Agnew in 1973, Ford was nominated by Nixon to be vice president. Confirmed by Congress, he became vice president on 6 December 1973. He became the nation's thirty-eighth president the following year when Nixon resigned on 9 August 1974. Ford is the first person in the history of the United States to be appointed to fill a vacancy in the vice presidency and the only vice president to become president upon the resignation of the president. As a consequence of his defeat by Jimmy Carter in the 1976 presidential election, he is also the only person to serve as both vice president and president who did not win election or reelection to either office.

EARLY YEARS. Born on 14 July 1913 in Omaha, Nebraska, the future president was named Leslie Lynch King Jr. after his father. His parents divorced when he was two years old, and he and his mother, Dorothy Ayer Gardner, returned to her parents' home in Grand Rapids, Michigan. There she met Gerald R. Ford, whom she married in 1916. Ford later adopted her young son, who took Ford's name.

Jerry Ford attended the Grand Rapids public schools and the University of Michigan, graduating in 1935. An all-star athlete, he received several offers to play professional football but chose to attend Yale Law School. Upon graduating in 1941, he returned to Grand Rapids to practice law. He joined the U.S. Navy in April 1942, served nearly four years and was discharged with the rank of lieutenant commander in January 1946.

Ford then returned to Grand Rapids and resumed his law practice. His real interest, however, was pol-

itics. He decided to run for Congress, challenging the local Republican incumbent in the 1948 primary election. A carefully planned campaign resulted in an upset victory in the primary and then an easy win in the November general election. Between the primary and the election, he married Elizabeth "Betty" Bloomer, a former dancer and fashion model. During the decade that followed, they had four children.

▲ *Congressman Ford stayed in close touch with the voters in his district. In 1955, he was in Hudsonville, Michigan.* (Courtesy National Archives.)

U.S. HOUSE OF REPRESENTATIVES. For 25 years, Ford represented Grand Rapids in the U.S. House of Representatives, winning reelection 12 times. Politically conservative, he opposed big government and the expansion of the federal government into areas such as education and health care. He was also committed to U.S. leadership abroad and to the expansion of the military to support this role. Ford took on broader party responsibilities in 1963, when his colleagues elected him chairman of the House Republican caucus. Two years later, eager to position himself to become Speaker, he ran for election as House minority leader, successfully unseating the incumbent. Now a major voice in Republican leadership, Ford became an outspoken critic of President Lyndon B. Johnson's Vietnam policies and of the costly social programs of the

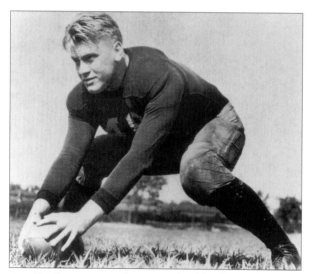

▲ *Ford was named most valuable player for the University of Michigan football team. He played in the College All-Star Game in 1935, the year of his graduation. The Detroit Lions and the Green Bay Packers both made offers to Ford to play professional football.* (Courtesy National Archives.)

The oath of office was administered to Gerald R. Ford by Chief Justice Warren E. Burger on 9 August 1974. His wife, Betty, was at his side. (Courtesy National Archives.)

Great Society. With Richard M. Nixon's election to the presidency in 1968, Ford expected a closer relationship with the White House. However, the Nixon administration had little interest in consulting with Republican congressional leaders. Ford was also disappointed when President Nixon's reelection landslide in 1972 failed to carry over into the congressional races and give the party control in the House. He resolved to continue as the House minority leader until 1977 and the conclusion of Nixon's second term.

Nixon and his White House staff, however, soon became involved in a major scandal. The scandal centered on charges that Nixon and his colleagues had tried to block the investigation of two burglaries at Democratic National Committee offices in the Watergate office and hotel complex in Washington, D.C., in the spring of 1972. Nixon denied knowledge of any cover-up attempts, but

investigations by a special federal prosecutor and congressional committees in 1973 and 1974 revealed that the White House was involved. This led to calls for Nixon's impeachment. During the same period, unrelated to Watergate, federal investigators charged Vice President Agnew with accepting bribes while serving as governor of Maryland and as vice president. Agnew resigned from office on 10 October 1973. Following procedures established by the Twenty-fifth Amendment to the Constitution, Nixon nominated Ford as the new vice president. Congress quickly confirmed the popular Michigan Republican, and he took the oath of office on 6 December 1973.

PRESIDENCY. For the next eight months, Ford served as Nixon's vice president and defended him, despite his own growing suspicions and concerns. The end came in August 1974 when Nixon, under court order, released tapes of Oval Office conversa-

On 8 September 1974, President Ford granted former President Richard M. Nixon a full pardon for all crimes he may have committed while in office. His approval ratings dropped sharply, and many never forgave him for his action. (Courtesy National Archives.)

tions that proved that he was involved in the cover-up. Nixon's impeachment in the House and his conviction in the Senate were now almost certain. Nixon announced on 8 August that he would resign. At noon on 9 August, Gerald Ford was sworn in as the thirty-eighth president of the United States.

The issue of what would happen to Nixon still remained. Many friends and former staff members urged the new president to grant Nixon a pardon. After many discussions, Ford announced on 8 September 1974 that he was granting Nixon a "full, free, and absolute pardon." This stopped any federal criminal or civil prosecution. Ford justified his decision as necessary to avoid a lengthy trial that would have divided the country. Public opinion polls, however, indicated that as many as 60 percent of Americans opposed the pardon.

Critics argued that Nixon should have been brought to trial or at least been made to admit his guilt as part of the terms of the pardon. Rumors circulated that the pardon was part of a deal between

Ford and Nixon to get Nixon to resign and avoid further embarrassment for the Republican Party. Eight days after the Nixon pardon, Ford announced an amnesty (pardon) program for Vietnam-era draft dodgers and deserters. In contrast to the Nixon pardon, however, the offer of amnesty was conditional, requiring up to two years public service. Only about 22,000 of the 106,000 individuals eligible applied for amnesty.

Ford was determined to put Watergate to rest and move on with the nation's business. One of his first responsibilities was to nominate a vice president. He chose Nelson A. Rockefeller, a former governor of New York, who took office in December 1974 after confirmation by Congress. For the first time in history, the nation's two highest offices were held by individuals who had not been elected to them. Wanting to maintain continuity, Ford at first kept Nixon's cabinet in place. However, by mid-1976, he had replaced all but three cabinet members. He also tried to be more

GRANTING PARDON TO RICHARD NIXON
BY THE PRESIDENT OF THE UNITED STATES
A PROCLAMATION

Richard Nixon became the thirty-seventh President of the United States on January 20, 1969 and was reelected in 1972 for a second term by the electors of forty-nine of the fifty states. His term in office continued until his resignation on August 9, 1974.

Pursuant to resolutions of the House of Representatives, its Committee on the Judiciary conducted an inquiry and investigation on the impeachment of the President extending over more than eight months. The hearings of the Committee and its deliberations, which received wide national publicity over television, radio, and in printed media, resulted in votes adverse to Richard Nixon on recommended Articles of Impeachment.

As a result of certain acts or omissions occurring before his resignation from the Office of President, Richard Nixon has become liable to possible indictment and trial for offenses against the United States. Whether or not he shall be so prosecuted depends on findings of the appropriate grand jury and on the discretion of the authorized prosecutor. Should an indictment ensue, the accused shall then be entitled to a fair trial by an impartial jury, as guaranteed to every individual by the Constitution.

It is believed that a trial of Richard Nixon, if it became necessary, could not fairly begin until a year or more has elapsed. In the meantime, the tranquillity to which this nation has been restored by the events of recent weeks could be irreparably lost by the prospects of bringing to trial a former President of the United States. The prospects of such trial will cause prolonged and divisive debate over the propriety of exposing to further punishment and degradation a man who has already paid the unprecedented penalty of relinquishing the highest elective office of the United States.

NOW, THEREFORE, I, Gerald R. Ford, President of the United States, pursuant to the pardon power conferred upon me by Article II, Section 2, of the Constitution, have granted and by these presents do grant a full, free, and absolute pardon unto Richard Nixon for all offenses against the United States which he, Richard Nixon, has committed or may have committed or taken part in during the period from January 20, 1969 through August 9, 1974. . . .

* *President Ford signed this pardon on 8 September 1974.*

---

open and accessible to counter the "imperial presidency" of the Nixon years, but access had its price. Two attempts to assassinate Ford were made within the month of September 1975.

DOMESTIC POLICY. Ford's domestic policy goals as president were the same as those he had advocated in Congress. He wanted to lessen federal government intervention in people's lives and to rely more on individual initiative and local responsi-

bility. The economy was the biggest problem facing the new president. When Ford took office, the rate of inflation was 12 percent; Ford identified that as "public enemy number 1." He called an economic summit in September to discuss ways to lower the inflation rate. The following month he announced a 10-point plan that included tax increases and spending cuts. By November it was clear that the most serious problem was not inflation but unemployment. The remedies Ford had proposed the previous month might make that problem even worse. As the nation slid into a recession and unemployment reached a postwar high of 9 percent, Ford reversed track and proposed to lower income taxes by $16 billion. Congress subsequently approved and Ford agreed to a slightly larger tax cut, modified at the insistence of the Democrats to provide more assistance to those in lower income brackets. The President remained firmly opposed, however, to increasing government spending in order to stimulate the economy and reduce unemployment. Instead, he called for reductions in government spending, particularly in domestic programs, to keep the deficit down. He vetoed more than 50 bills that called for more government spending. Although these actions and others to reduce U.S. dependence on foreign oil put the economy on firmer footing, recovery was slow. By October 1976, just before the general election, unemployment still stood at about 8 percent, and there were indications that the recovery was slowing down.

FOREIGN POLICY. Ford asked Secretary of State Henry Kissinger to stay on in that post. Ford relied on the veteran diplomat as he faced crises in Cyprus, the Middle East, Angola, and Southeast Asia. He completed the U.S. withdrawal from Vietnam that had been begun by Nixon. Facing the likelihood that Saigon, the South Vietnamese capital, would fall to the approaching North Vietnamese troops, Ford first asked Congress to provide $722 million in military aid and $250 million for social and economic aid to help the failing South Vietnamese Government. In April 1975, after Congress refused to provide the requested aid, he felt he had no choice but to order the emergency evacuation of both the remaining U.S. troops and civilians and those South Vietnamese who had fought on the side of or cooperated with the U.S.

Cambodia presented a bigger problem. Less than a month after seizing the Cambodian capital city of Phnom Penh, Cambodian troops captured a

President Ford met with Egyptian President Anwar Sadat in Austria on 2 June 1975. Four months later, Israel and Egypt signed a peace agreement. (Courtesy National Archives.)

26

U.S. merchant ship, the *Mayaguez*, and its 40-man crew in the Gulf of Thailand. Concerned about potential damage to U.S. prestige and power, Ford called the seizure an act of piracy. After efforts to negotiate the crew's release failed, he ordered the Marines to attack the island of Koh Tang, where the crew was reportedly being held. Forty-one Americans were killed and 50 wounded in what turned out to be an unnecessary action. The Cambodians had already decided to release the crew and had removed them from the island.

Ford shared Nixon's commitment to détente (easing of tensions) with the Soviet Union but found both Democratic and Republican congressional support failing. In late 1974, for example, the Senate amended the Trade Reform bill to make most favored nation status for the Soviet Union dependent on the Soviets allowing Jews to emigrate. The Soviets refused, stalling efforts to open up trade between the two nations. Relations became worse in 1975 when the two powers took opposing sides in the Angolan civil war. Nevertheless, Ford still hoped to secure a new strategic arms limitations treaty. In July 1975, he met with Soviet leader Leonid Brezhnev in Helsinki, Finland. Although the two leaders did not agree on many things, they did agree to support a declaration of 10 principles signed by the 35 nations participating in the Helsinki Conference on Security and Cooperation in Europe. Critics insisted that the Helsinki Agreement, in recognizing post–World War II boundaries in Eastern Europe, approved Soviet dominance there. Ford and his supporters empha-

President Ford met with Soviet General Secretary Leonid Brezhnev in Vladivostock, U.S.S.R. in November 1974. Their talks laid the groundwork for a new SALT (Strategic Arms Limited Treaty) agreement. (Courtesy National Archives.)

sized provisions calling for humanitarian and cultural cooperation and freer movement of people and ideas across borders.

REELECTION BID. Despite earlier doubts, Ford decided to run for a full term in 1976. His chief Republican opponent was Ronald Reagan, a former governor of California and an extremely popular figure among party conservatives. The two fought it out in primaries across the nation. Ford narrowly won the nomination on the first ballot at the GOP convention in August 1976. Rockefeller

▲ *President Ford and Jimmy Carter had three debates. The second debate, in San Francisco on 6 October 1976, was on foreign affairs. Ford was very aware of criticism about the Helsinki Conference, and he mistakenly said that there was "no Soviet domination in Eastern Europe." This cast doubt in the minds of many voters about Ford's knowledge of foreign affairs.* (Courtesy National Archives.)

had resigned, so Ford chose Kansas Senator Robert Dole as his running mate. He went on to face the Democratic candidate, Jimmy Carter, a former governor of Georgia. Although hindered by both continuing high unemployment and continuing popular resentment over the Nixon pardon, Ford waged a strong campaign. His only serious mistake came in a series of televised national debates, the first since the famous Kennedy-Nixon debates in 1960. Although Carter carried only 23 states and the District of Columbia, he received 1.7 million more popular votes, winning 297 electoral votes to Ford's 240. Thus came another addition to Gerald Ford's list of "firsts": He became the first president in 44 years to be turned out of office by voters.

After leaving the White House, Ford published his memoirs, *A Time to Heal*, lectured widely, and served on the boards of directors of several companies. In 1981, the Gerald R. Ford Museum opened in Grand Rapids and the Gerald R. Ford Library opened in Ann Arbor, Michigan.

▲ *Jerry and Betty Ford retired to Palm Springs, California in 1977. Ten years later he said, "I have competed enough in life and, whether it is athletics or politics or law, I know that sometimes you win and sometimes you lose."* (Courtesy National Archives.)

VICE PRESIDENT

Nelson Aldrich Rockefeller
(1908–1979)

CHRONOLOGICAL EVENTS

1908	Born, Bar Harbor, Maine, 8 July
1930	Graduated from Dartmouth College, New Hampshire
1940	Appointed director of the Office of Inter-American Affairs
1953	Appointed under secretary of health, education, and welfare
1958	Elected governor of New York
1974	Appointed vice president
1979	Died, New York, New York, 26 January

BIOGRAPHY

A grandson of John D. Rockefeller, the founder of the Standard Oil Company, Nelson Rockefeller was born into enormous wealth. He grew up in a New York townhouse filled with his parents' art collections. Dyslexia (a learning disorder) complicated Rockefeller's early education, but he graduated Phi Beta Kappa from Dartmouth.

During the 1930s, Rockefeller helped direct his family's vast financial empire, from Rockefeller Center in New York to an oil company in Venezuela. He was also treasurer of the Museum of Modern Art in New York. During World War II, Rockefeller coordinated U.S. policies in Latin America and played a role in the creation of the United Nations. Under President Dwight Eisenhower, he became secretary of the new Department of Health, Education, and Welfare.

Rockefeller defeated another millionaire, Averell Harriman, to win election as governor of New York in 1958. In four terms as governor, he built an impressive record of accomplishments, all the while repeatedly campaigning for the Republican presidential nomination. In 1960, he lost the nomination to Richard Nixon but forced Nixon to accept a more liberal party platform. In 1964, he was defeated by the conservative Arizona Senator Barry Goldwater. In 1968, he again lost to Nixon.

Rockefeller resigned during his fourth term as governor to head a Commission on Critical Choices for America. Many expected him to try again for the presidency in 1976. When Nixon resigned because of the Watergate scandal, President Gerald Ford appointed Rockefeller vice president under the Twenty-fifth Amendment. A long Senate investigation into Rockefeller's finances delayed his confirmation for months.

Ford appointed his vice president to chair a commission to investigate the CIA's domestic spying. Rockefeller also headed the President's Domestic Council and created a science advisory unit. Yet while Rockefeller met weekly with the President, he was rarely consulted in advance on the administration's policy-making decisions.

Facing a challenge for the presidential nomination in 1976 from party conservatives, Ford dropped Rockefeller from the ticket. After losing the election to the Democratic nominee, Jimmy Carter of Georgia, Ford called his abandonment of Rockefeller "the biggest political mistake of my life." Retiring from politics, Rockefeller devoted the rest of his life to his interest in art.

THE CABINET

SECRETARY OF STATE
Henry A. Kissinger, 1974

SECRETARY OF THE TREASURY
William E. Simon, 1974

ATTORNEY GENERAL
William B. Saxbe, 1974
Edward H. Levi, 1975

SECRETARY OF THE INTERIOR
Rogers C.B. Morton, 1974
Stanley K. Hathaway, 1975
Thomas S. Kleppe, 1975

SECRETARY OF AGRICULTURE
Earl L. Butz, 1974
John A. Knebel, 1976

SECRETARY OF COMMERCE
Frederick B. Dent, 1974
Rogers C.B. Morton, 1975
Elliot L. Richardson, 1976

SECRETARY OF LABOR
Peter J. Brennan, 1974
John T. Dunlop, 1975
W. J. Usery, Jr., 1976

SECRETARY OF DEFENSE
James R. Schlesinger, 1974
Donald H. Rumsfeld, 1975

SECRETARY OF HEALTH, EDUCATION, AND WELFARE
Caspar W. Weinburger, 1974
F. David Mathews, 1975

SECRETARY OF HOUSING AND URBAN DEVELOPMENT
James T. Lynn, 1974
Carla Anderson Hills, 1975

SECRETARY OF TRANSPORTATION
Claude S. Brinegar, 1974
William T. Coleman, Jr., 1975

Carla A. Hills is shown here with President Ford in the Oval Office on 24 March 1975. (Courtesy Gerald R. Ford Library.)

Carla A. Hills (1934–). Hills was appointed secretary of housing and urban development by President Gerald R. Ford in 1975. She had previously served as head of the Civil Division, Department of Justice, (1974). Hills was the first woman to serve as assistant attorney general in 40 years.

As secretary of housing and urban development, Hills was a tough and efficient administrator. In 1978, she returned to her law practice in Los Angeles, California. She is a former president of the Women's Lawyer Association. She is co-author of Federal Civil Practice and editor and co-author of Antitrust Advisor.

In 1989, Hills was appointed U.S. trade representative by President George Bush.

Henry Kissinger is shown with President Ford and Vice President Nelson A. Rockefeller in the Oval Office. September 1974. (Courtesy Library of Congress.)

Henry Kissinger (1923–). Kissinger was appointed secretary of state by President Richard M. Nixon in 1973. He had previously served as Nixon's national security advisor (1968–1973). He spent two years negotiating a cease-fire in Vietnam, which was announced on the eve of the 1972 presidential election and signed in Paris on 23 January 1973. He received the 1973 Nobel Peace Prize for his role in the negotiation.

Kissinger retained his post in the administration of Gerald R. Ford. His frequent travels to many countries introduced a new phrase, "shuttle diplomacy." In 1974, he helped negotiate the Egyptian-Israeli Disengagement Agreement. The two countries agreed not to use war as a means of settling disputes.

During his tenure as secretary of state, Kissinger also met with southern African leaders to discuss black majority rule in Rhodesia and independence for South African-controlled Namibia. In 1977, he was awarded the Presidential Medal of Freedom.

FAMILY

CHRONOLOGICAL EVENTS

8 April 1918	Elizabeth Anne (Betty) Bloomer born	15 October 1948	Betty Bloomer married Gerry Ford
1942	Betty Bloomer married William C. Warren	14 March 1950	Son, Michael Gerald (Mike), born
		16 March 1952	Son, John (Jack), born
1947	Betty Bloomer divorced William C. Warren	19 May 1956	Son, Steven Meigs (Steve), born
		6 July 1957	Daughter, Susan Elizabeth, born

Betty Ford appeared at the Republican Convention in 1976. This picture shows her acknowledging the thunderous applause which she received. (Courtesy Library of Congress.)

Elizabeth Anne Bloomer grew up in Grand Rapids, Michigan. She studied dance with Martha Graham in New York for two years and worked as a model for the Powers agency at the same time. She moved back to Grand Rapids in 1941 and taught dance to disabled children. She married Gerry Ford in 1948, two weeks before he won his first election to the United States Congress.

In 1973, Mrs. Ford found herself at the center of public attention as the First Lady. She used her own experience with breast cancer to make other women aware of the importance of detecting the disease as early as possible. She received more than 50,000 letters and cards in the weeks after her operation. Many were from women who had had similar operations.

After her family left the White House, she made public her dependency on alcohol and prescription drugs in two books: *The Times of My Life* and *Betty: A Glad Awakening.* She is president of the Betty Ford Clinic at the Eisenhower Medical Center in California. Mrs. Ford speaks often on alcoholism and its treatment and on breast cancer.

After the problems of Watergate, Mrs. Ford helped to restore national confidence in the presidency. She spoke with dignity, humor, and honesty. She was a devoted follower of the Equal Rights Amendment. Betty Ford is a woman of great courage who reassured the American people that families and feminism can go together.

The Fords had three sons and a daughter. They are shown here with Steve and Susan feeding Flag, a deer at Camp David, in 1974. Steve decided not to attend Duke University when his father was elected president. He has worked in a rodeo and had parts in TV shows and movies. In 1994, he resigned as associate vice president of Turfway Park, Kentucky.

Susan married a Secret Service agent, but they divorced after 10 years. She is now remarried and living in Tulsa. She flies over 60,000 miles and does 50 to 60 interviews a year on behalf of breast cancer awareness.

Mike attended Gordon-Conwell Theological Seminary in Massachusetts and is director of student development at Wake Forest University, Winston-Salem, North Carolina.

Jack graduated from Utah State University. He was executive director of the committee responsible for raising $11.2 million for the 1996 Republic National Convention in San Diego, California. (Courtesy Gerald R. Ford Library.)

GERALD R. FORD HOUSE

514 Crown View Drive • Alexandria, Virginia 22314

> *The home is privately owned and not open to the public.*

The Fords built the two-story brick house in 1955. They lived there during most of Gerald Ford's 25 years as a congressman, until August 1974, when he assumed the presidency. It was sold to a private owner in January 1977. Although the house was awarded National Historic Landmark status in December 1985, it is privately owned and not open to the public.

The Ford family lived in Alexandria, Virginia from 1955 to 1974. (Courtesy Gerald R. Ford Library.)

THE GERALD R. FORD MUSEUM

303 Pearl Street, NW • Grand Rapids, Michigan 49504 • Tel: (616) 451-9263

> *Located on the Grand River, next to the downtown conference center. Open daily from 9 A.M. to 4:45 P.M. Closed Thanksgiving, Christmas, and New Year's Day. Admission fee. Children and school groups admitted free. Group tours available; advance arrangements encouraged. For school tours, grades 5 through 12, contact the Education Specialist two weeks in advance; call: (616) 456-2675. Three wheelchairs are available at the admissions desk of the museum. Gift shop open during regular hours. Operated by the National Archives and Records Administration.*

The museum is only a short walk from the site of Ford's first campaign headquarters. It is a granite and glass triangular structure which houses Ford memorabilia and exhibits. The exhibits feature his congressional years, vice-presidency, pardon of Nixon, 1976 presidential campaign, and related national and international issues. A full-scale reproduction of the Oval Office is also on the site.

On 18 September 1981, Ford dedicated the Gerald R. Ford Museum to the American People. (Courtesy Gerald R. Ford Library.)

34

THE GERALD R. FORD LIBRARY

1000 Beal Avenue • Ann Arbor, Michigan 48109 • Tel: (313) 668-2218

Located on the North Campus of the University of Michigan at Ann Arbor. Open Monday through Friday, except on federal holidays, from 8:45 A.M. to 4:45 P.M. Saturday mornings and occasional after-hour visits are sometimes available by advance appointment. No admission fee. Administered by the National Archives and Records Administration.

The Gerald R. Ford Library is 130 miles from the Ford Museum. (Courtesy Gerald R. Ford Library.)

The Gerald R. Ford Library and Museum are unique among the nation's presidential libraries in that they are separated by 130 miles. The split location is a compromise between competing claims on Ford's loyalties. The library is located on the Ann Arbor campus of the University of Michigan, which Ford attended, and the museum overlooks the Grand River in Grand Rapids, Ford's boyhood hometown. Both buildings—built with private funds—were opened to the public in 1981. Despite their physical separation, the library and museum are joined as a single institution under one director.

The library houses Ford's presidential papers and research collections relating to his public life. Before Ford left the presidency, he donated all of his congressional, vice-presidential, and presidential historic materials, including the files of his White House staff. PRESNET, an automated database, is used to research the 20 million pages of papers and the half million audiovisual records now in the library. The database contains more than 55,000 folder titles and other descriptions of historic material. The collections not only reflect Ford's political career, but also represent many aspects of modern American society, business, and culture.

Jimmy Carter

39ᵀᴴ PRESIDENT
OF THE UNITED STATES OF AMERICA

CHRONOLOGICAL EVENTS

1 October 1924	Born, Plains, Georgia
5 June 1946	Graduated from U.S. Naval Academy at Annapolis
1946–1953	Served in U.S. Navy
1953	Returned to Georgia to manage family peanut farm
6 November 1962	Elected to Georgia State Senate
3 November 1964	Reelected to Georgia State Senate
1966	Ran unsuccessfully for governor of Georgia
3 November 1970	Elected governor of Georgia
2 November 1976	Elected president
20 January 1977	Inaugurated president
21 January 1977	Pardoned Vietnam War draft evaders
7 September 1977	Panama Canal Treaty signed; ratified by U.S. Senate in 1978
1 October 1977	Established Department of Energy
17 September 1978	Camp David Agreements signed
November 1978	Secured Congressional approval of national energy program
15 December 1978	Announced full diplomatic relations with China; effective 1 January 1979
17 October 1979	Established Department of Education
26 March 1979	Israeli-Egyptian peace treaty signed
March 1979	Three Mile Island nuclear accident
18 June 1979	Signed SALT II Treaty
4 November 1979	U.S. embassy workers in Iran taken hostage
23 January 1980	Announced Carter Doctrine
24 April 1980	Dispatched armed rescue mission to free hostages in Iran
20 February 1980	Announced U.S. boycott of Olympic Games in Moscow to protest the Soviet invasion of Afghanistan
4 November 1980	Defeated for reelection as president
20 January 1981	U.S. hostages released by Iran
	Retired to Plains, Georgia
1982	Published memoirs, *Keeping Faith: Memoirs of a President*
1985	Published memoirs, *The Blood of Abraham*

BIOGRAPHY

In September 1973 Jimmy Carter told his mother that, when he completed his term as governor of Georgia, he planned to run for president. Her response was, "President of what?" That Carter's own mother did not think of him in terms of the presidency of the United States is evidence of just how surprising his ambitious goal was. Relatively unknown outside his native Georgia, he nevertheless went on to win the Democratic nomination in 1976 and election as the nation's thirty-ninth president.

James Earl Carter, Jr. was born in Plains, Georgia, on 1 October 1924. Jimmy, as he was always called, grew up and went to school in the small rural community where his father farmed and ran a small peanut warehouse business and his mother worked as a registered nurse. In 1943, he achieved a childhood dream when he entered the U.S. Naval Academy at Annapolis. After graduating from the Academy in 1946, he married Rosalynn Smith, a young woman from Plains who was his sister's best friend. The Carters had four children—three sons (John, James, and Jeffrey) and a daughter, Amy.

Carter began his naval service after Annapolis as an electronics instructor. He had advanced to the position of engineering officer in the nuclear submarine program by the time he resigned his commission in 1953. He returned to Plains to take over the family's businesses after the death of his father. During the next decade he proved himself to be a shrewd businessman, expanding the peanut farm and warehouse business into a thriving and profitable operation.

EARLY POLITICAL CAREER. Interested in public service, he became active in local school board politics and then, in 1962, successfully ran for a seat in the Georgia State Senate. He won reelection to a second two-year term in 1964 and established a reputation for being conservative on fiscal matters but liberal on social issues such as civil rights. He ambitiously set his sights on the Georgia governorship but was defeated in the Democratic primary in his first try in 1966. Demonstrating the persistence and competitive

Jimmy Carter graduated 59th in a class of 820 from the United States Naval Academy at Annapolis in 1946. He served in the navy until 1953, when he returned to Plains, Georgia to take over the family business. (Courtesy Jimmy Carter Library.)

nature that would characterize his later campaigns, he made a second try for the position in 1970. He easily won both the primary and the general election appealing, despite his earlier social liberalism, to conservative white voters. Given the tone of his campaign, his 1971 gubernatorial inaugural address proved surprising, for in it he explicitly called for an end to racial segregation. The speech focused national attention on Carter, who was widely hailed as the leader of a new breed of moderate politicians in the New South.

As governor, Carter followed through on his inaugural promises. During his tenure, the percentage of African American state employees rose by 40 percent, and the number of black appointees rose from 3 to 53. His real focus, however, was on making the state government more efficient, and toward that end he established zero-based budgeting—ending assumptions of continued funding and requiring agencies to justify every budget request—and consolidated 300 agencies and offices into 22.

ELECTION OF 1976. Carter was prohibited under the Georgia constitution from running for a second consecutive term as governor. He decided to run for the presidency and announced his candidacy in December 1974, a month before the end of his term as governor. He was convinced that as a political outsider he could overcome the voters' post-Watergate suspicion of politics as usual. He believed that he could provide the moral leadership he believed the nation needed. As he campaigned across the country over the next two years, he emphasized his personal character. He pledged that he would never lie to the American people, and that he was committed to open gov-

Carter's inaugural address as governor in 1971 called for an end to racial segregation. He is shown here with Dr. Martin Luther King, Sr., father of the slain civil rights leader. Dr. King, a lifelong Republican, supported Carter's campaign for the presidency. He delivered the benediction at the Democratic convention in July 1976. (Courtesy Jimmy Carter Library.)

ernment, but he was often deliberately vague on issues. As late as January 1976, a poll of Democratic voters reported that only 4 percent would choose him as the party's candidate. He continued on, planning to capitalize on changes in the delegate selection process that lessened the power of the established party hierarchy. He entered every primary except West Virginia's, building on an early win in the Iowa caucuses to capture the New Hampshire and Florida primaries. While his closest competitor won only 4 primaries, Carter won 17. This not only secured the all-important delegate votes but also established himself as a national political figure and an impressive vote-getter. He won the Democratic nomination on the first ballot at the party's national convention. He chose as his running mate Walter Mondale, then a U.S. senator from Minnesota and a popular figure with labor and the party's liberal wing. Although the

Jimmy and Rosalynn Carter walked down Pennsylvania Avenue to the White House after taking the oath of office at the Capitol. They did this as a way of rejecting the "imperial presidency" of Richard M. Nixon. (Courtesy Jimmy Carter Library.)

incumbent president, Gerald R. Ford, proved a stronger candidate than expected, Carter managed to gather sufficient support in the South and the East to secure a narrow victory. He won with only 50.1 percent of the popular vote and 297 electoral votes compared to Ford's 240 electoral votes.

Carter viewed his election as a rejection of the "imperial presidency" that had led to Watergate and immediately set about to establish a more populist style. After taking the oath of office at the Capitol, he walked to the White House rather than riding in a limousine. That symbolic gesture was followed by many others, including selling the presidential yacht, cutting out the trumpeters and other trappings of ceremony, and conducting casual radio programs dressed for photographs in a cardigan sweater. He also tried to use his appointive powers to bring greater diversity to government. Carter appointed two women to his cabinet (more than any of his predecessors had), and nearly a third of the circuit and district judges appointed during his tenure were women, African Americans or Hispanics.

Carter was convinced that post-Watergate America demanded a completely new kind of leadership from its president. He saw himself as a trustee for the public good, above the partisanship that had characterized his predecessors' terms in office. When this belief translated into a refusal to compromise or to work within the political system, he came into conflict with his own party's leadership in Congress. Although the Democrats controlled both houses of Congress, that did not ensure support for Carter's agenda. Former President Richard M. Nixon had tried to monopolize decision making. As a result, Congress became collectively determined to reassert its power in relationship to the White House and individually less inclined to follow the party line.

DOMESTIC AFFAIRS. Carter's record in domestic matters includes both successes—for example, the establishment of federal departments of energy and education, civil service reform, and deregulation of the airline industry—and failures—the defeat of national health insurance, welfare reform, and tax reform. But the problems between Carter and the Democratic Congress surfaced most clearly in regard to resolving the nation's economic problems. In the 1976 campaign, Carter had criticized President Gerald Ford, the Republican incumbent, for not controlling inflation and lowering unemployment. By the time of his inauguration, with the recession easing but unemployment still at 7.7 percent, Carter narrowed his agenda to focus on the threat of revived inflation. He pledged to eliminate what he considered its major cause—the federal budget deficit. His administration's economic policies thus emphasized traditional anti-inflationary measures that critics claimed failed to address fully the unemployment problem. The nation slipped by the last half of 1977 into what observers tagged "stagflation"—low economic growth accompanied by continued high inflation. Many of Carter's fellow Democrats in Congress found the President's proposals too conservative and unresponsive to the needs of the poor, minorities, and other traditional Democratic supporters hurt by the chronic shortage of jobs. By late 1979, the economy seemed to be spinning out of control, and in January 1980, inflation climbed to a staggering annual rate of 18.2 percent, while unemployment remained at 7 percent. Although inflation began to slow by mid-year, unemployment rose to 7.8 percent and was expected to climb higher by the end of the year. Recognizing that his policy was not popular politically, Carter, at the Democratic Party's presidential nominating convention in August, yielded to demands for platform planks that stated the Democrats' opposition to any actions that would worsen unemployment. Despite his promises in the 1976 election, Carter could claim no improvement in the economy by the time of the fall 1980 general election. Indeed, the rate of inflation, which had been 4.8 percent in 1976, hovered at 12 percent in the fall of 1980, while unemployment remained essentially unchanged at 7.7 percent.

A major contributor to the nation's economic woes was its dependence on foreign oil, which grew from 35 to 50 percent of the nation's total supply, even as the price doubled between 1973 and 1977. To counter both Americans' wasteful consumption of energy and the decline of domestic sources, Carter proposed a comprehensive energy program to limit imported oil, gradually end government price controls, and develop conservation programs and alternative energy sources, including an ambitious synthetic fuels program. Although Congress enacted much of the Carter program in 1978 and 1980—perhaps Carter's most impressive domestic policy achievement—oil imports and prices remained high, contributing to inflation. Carter combined his goal to reduce U.S. consumption of imported oil with the need for revenue to balance the budget. He proposed in March 1980 an oil import fee of 10 cents per gallon. Congress balked and overrode his veto of a joint resolution blocking the surcharge—the first time in nearly three decades that a Democratic Congress had overridden a Democratic president and a clear indication of Carter's eroding political capital.

FOREIGN AFFAIRS. In his 1976 campaign,

Carter had criticized the "secretive Lone Ranger" approach to foreign policy that had characterized the Nixon-Ford years. He had emphasized the need for open diplomacy and support for human rights through control of U.S. aid and exports. As president, he encountered conservative criticism for finalizing treaties relinquishing U.S. control over the Panama Canal and for establishing full

> "The other decision was to include in my State of the Union speech on January 23 a warning to the Soviets concerning any further threat by them against the Persian Gulf.
>
> *Let our position be absolutely clear: An attempt by any outside force to gain control of the Persian Gulf region will be regarded as an assault on the vital interests of the United States of America, and such an assault will be repelled by any means necessary, including military force.*
>
> This statement was not lightly made, and I was resolved to use the full power of the United States to back it up. I had already discussed my concerns about the Persian Gulf area with the Soviet leaders during the Vienna summit conference in June 1979, but their subsequent invasion of Afghanistan made it necessary to repeat the warning in clearer terms. Some news reporters dubbed my decision the Carter Doctrine and called it an idle threat, because, they said, we could not successfully invade Iran if it were attacked by Soviet troops."
>
> • *Jimmy Carter,* Keeping Faith: Memoirs of a President.

President Carter invited President Anwar Sadat of Egypt (left) and Prime Minister Menachem Begin of Israel to Camp David in September 1978. After 13 days of negotiation, they signed agreements that led to peace between Egypt and Israel. (Courtesy Jimmy Carter Library.)

diplomatic relations with China (and hence cutting formal ties with the Nationalist Chinese Government in Taiwan). He found broader support for his foreign policy initiatives than for his handling of domestic issues. Continuing efforts begun by his predecessors, he successfully negotiated with the Soviet Union a treaty limiting nuclear weapons (the second Strategic Arms Limitation Treaty, or SALT II), despite continuing tension caused by the Soviet Union's treatment of political dissidents. When the Soviets invaded Afghanistan in December 1979, however, he asked the U.S. Senate to suspend consideration of ratification and called for a U.S. boycott of the 1980 Summer Olympic Games in Moscow. The tensions with the Soviet Union provided the context for Carter's decision in July 1980 to initiate the largest arms procurement program in 30 years, despite his campaign promise to cut defense expenditures.

The high point for the Carter administration diplomatically came on 26 March 1979, when

Israel and Egypt signed a peace treaty, a historic first step in resolving long-standing problems in the Middle East. Credit for this went to the Carter administration, since the treaty was based on agreements reached between representatives of the two nations at meetings initiated by the White House and held the previous fall at Camp David, the presidential retreat in Maryland. Although the treaty was vague and implementation proved difficult, it still constituted an important achievement that had eluded others for three decades.

Carter also encountered his biggest problem in the Middle East—specifically, in Iran. In January 1979, Islamic fundamentalists under the leadership of Ayatollah Ruhollah Khomeini overthrew the Shah of Iran. The United States continued its support of the deposed Shah. In October 1979 Carter agreed to allow the Shah into the United States for cancer treatment. Then, on 2 November 1979, militants claiming to be Iranian students seized the U. S. embassy in Teheran and took more than 50

CAMP DAVID AGREEMENTS

When we first arrived at Camp David, the first thing upon which we agreed was to ask the people of the world to pray that our negotiations would be successful. Those prayers have been answered far beyond any expectations. We are privileged to witness tonight a significant achievement in the cause of peace, an achievement none thought possible a year ago, or even a month ago, an achievement that reflects the courage and wisdom of these two leaders.

Through thirteen long days at Camp David, we have seen them display determination and vision and flexibility which was needed to make this agreement come to pass. All of us owe them our gratitude and respect. They know that they will always have my personal admiration.

There are still great difficulties that remain and many hard issues to be settled. The questions that have brought warfare and bitterness to the Middle East for the last thirty years will not be settled overnight. But we should all recognize the substantial achievements that have been made.

One of the agreements that President Sadat and Prime Minister Begin are signing tonight is entitled, "A Framework For Peace in the Middle East."

This framework concerns the principles and some specifics in the most substantive way which will govern a comprehensive peace settlement. It deals specifically with the future of the West Bank and Gaza, and the need to resolve the Palestinian problem in all its aspects. The framework document proposes a five-year transitional period in the West Bank and Gaza during which the Israeli military government will be withdrawn and a self-governing authority will be elected with full autonomy.

It also provides for Israeli forces to remain in specified locations during this period to protect Israel's security.

The Palestinians will have the right to participate in the determination of their own future, in negotiations which will resolve the final status of the West Bank and Gaza, and then to produce an Israeli-Jordanian treaty. . . .

Well, the long days at Camp David are over. But many months of difficult negotiation still lie ahead.

I hope that the foresight and the wisdom that have made this session a success will guide these leaders and the leaders of all nations as they continue the progress toward peace.

• *President Carter delivered these comments on 17 September 1978. He announced an agreement on the framework for peace in the Middle East, and for a peace treaty between Egypt and Israel. The peace treaty between Egypt and Israel was signed six months later.*

Americans hostage, demanding that the United States return the Shah to Iran for trial. While seeking a diplomatic resolution to the crisis, Carter cut off all U.S. oil purchases from Iran and froze Iranian assets in the United States. When those efforts proved unproductive, Carter formally broke off diplomatic relations with Iran and in late April 1980 approved an armed rescue attempt. The failure of the raid increased the public's frustration over the prolonged crisis and hurt Carter politically as he faced reelection that fall. (Ironically, in return for the unfreezing of Iranian assets and other concessions, the hostages were finally freed on 20 January 1981, the day that Carter's successor was inaugurated.)

ELECTION OF 1980. By mid-1979, Carter's reelection prospects seemed dim. The White House appeared to be in disarray: Carter dismissed four

The Iranian leader, Ayatollah Ruhollah Khomeini, released the U.S. hostages on the day that President Carter's successor, Ronald Reagan, was inaugurated. (Courtesy Ronald Reagan Library.)

cabinet members (and accepted the resignation of a fifth), several close aides were investigated for wrongdoing, and the President's brother, Billy, was charged with receiving funds as an unregistered lobbyist for Libya. In a public opinion poll conducted in October 1979 regarding the leadership abilities of various potential Democratic and Republican presidential candidates, Carter came in dead last. The following month, Massachusetts Senator Edward M. Kennedy—the highest-ranked contender in the poll—announced that he would challenge Carter for the Democratic nomination. Although Carter managed to hold onto the nomination by defeating Kennedy in 24 out of 34 primaries in the winter and spring of 1980, he appeared to have little chance of winning the general election. In July, the Gallup Poll reported that Carter's approval rating was 21 percent, the lowest of any president, including Nixon at the time of his resignation, since the company began polling in 1936. But despite the division within the party caused by Kennedy's candidacy and Carter's low

approval rating, the President still managed to mount a strong campaign against his Republican opponent, Ronald Reagan, the former governor of California. Although polls predicted an even contest in the last days of the campaign, Reagan won in a landslide with 51 percent of the popular vote, compared to Carter's 42 percent and 7 percent for the third-party candidate John Anderson. The magnitude of Reagan's win was even clearer in the Electoral College—he won 489 votes to Carter's 49.

After his defeat, Carter returned to Plains, where he wrote his memoirs, *Keeping Faith* (1982) and *The Blood of Abraham* (1985), and became active in Habitat for Humanity, a nonprofit organization that builds houses for the poor. He founded the Carter Center in 1982, at Emory University in nearby Atlanta. In 1986, the Jimmy Carter Library opened there. In his role as elder statesman, he has traveled around the world, helping to resolve election disputes and other situations, and is recognized as an effective advocate for international peace, social justice, and political democracy.

VICE PRESIDENT

Walter Frederick Mondale
(1928–)

CHRONOLOGICAL EVENTS

1928	Born, Ceylon, Minnesota, 5 January
1951	Graduated from University of Minnesota
1951	Enlisted in the U.S. Army
1960	Appointed Minnesota attorney general
1964	Appointed to U.S. Senate
1976	Elected vice president
1984	Ran unsuccessfully for president
1993	Appointed U.S. ambassador to Japan

BIOGRAPHY

Walter Frederick "Fritz" Mondale was born in Ceylon, Minnesota, the son of a Methodist minister and a music teacher. As a student, Mondale volunteered to work in the campaigns of Minneapolis's liberal mayor Hubert Humphrey. After serving in the army and finishing law school, he resumed active participation in Minnesota's Democratic-Farmer-Labor Party. Mondale's success in managing Orville Freeman's campaign for governor gained

him appointment as the nation's youngest state attorney general. His efforts for consumer protection and civil rights helped him win election as attorney general in his own right.

When Humphrey was elected vice president in 1964, Mondale was appointed to fill his seat in the U.S. Senate. He supported both Lyndon Johnson's "Great Society" and the war in Vietnam. After the Republican Richard M. Nixon became president, Mondale opposed continuing the war and helped pass the War Powers Resolution to limit presidential power to make war.

Planning to run for president in 1976, Mondale traveled widely, speaking, building a campaign staff, and raising funds. But in November 1974, he withdrew from the race, explaining that he lacked "the overwhelming desire to be president" or to spend two more years "sleeping in Holiday Inns." The Democratic nomination went to a Washington outsider, former Georgia Governor Jimmy Carter. Seeking a compatible running mate with federal experience, Carter chose Mondale. After winning a close election, Mondale became the first vice president to move along with his family, into the vice presidential mansion.

The President and Vice President formed such a team that some of Carter's conservative supporters complained that the liberal Mondale was shaping the administration's policies and appointments. Mondale played adviser and troubleshooter. While he never challenged the President's authority, he often felt frustrated by Carter's inept handling of Congress and his inability to define his positions. Carter steadily lost public favor and was defeated for reelection in 1980 by former California Governor Ronald Reagan.

Mondale ran for president in 1984. He won acclaim for selecting New York Representative Geraldine Ferraro for vice president, but he blundered by supporting an increase in taxes. Nor could his dry public image match the telegenic Reagan, who swept 49 states to win election. Mondale resumed practicing law until he became U.S. ambassador to Japan in 1993.

THE CABINET

SECRETARY OF STATE
Cyrus R. Vance, 1977
Edmund S. Muskie, 1980

SECRETARY OF THE TREASURY
W. Michael Blumenthal, 1977
G. William Miller, 1979

ATTORNEY GENERAL
Griffin B. Bell, 1977
Benjamin R. Civiletti, 1979

SECRETARY OF THE INTERIOR
Cecil D. Andrus, 1977

SECRETARY OF AGRICULTURE
Bob S. Bergland, 1977

SECRETARY OF COMMERCE
Juanita M. Kreps, 1977
Philip M. Klutznick, 1980

SECRETARY OF LABOR
Ray F. Marshall, 1977

SECRETARY OF DEFENSE
Harold Brown, 1977

SECRETARY OF HEALTH, EDUCATION, AND WELFARE[1]
Joseph A. Califano, Jr., 1977
Patricia Roberts Harris, 1979

SECRETARY OF HOUSING AND URBAN DEVELOPMENT
Patricia Roberts Harris, 1977
Moon Landrieu, 1979

SECRETARY OF TRANSPORTATION
Brock Adams, 1977
Neil E. Goldschmidt, 1979

SECRETARY OF ENERGY[2]
James R. Schlesinger, 1977
Charles W. Duncan, 1979

SECRETARY OF HEALTH AND HUMAN SERVICES[1]
Patricia Roberts Harris, 1979

SECRETARY OF EDUCATION[1]
Shirley M. Hufstedler, 1979

1. Department divided (17 October 1979) into Department of Education and Department of Health and Human Services.
2. Department of Energy established 4 August 1977.

Patricia Roberts Harris is shown here taking the oath of office as secretary of health, education, and welfare on 3 August 1979. (Courtesy Jimmy Carter Library.)

Patricia Roberts Harris (1924–1985). Harris was appointed secretary of housing and urban development by President Jimmy Carter in 1977. She had previously served as ambassador to Luxembourg during the administration of Lyndon B. Johnson.

As secretary of housing and urban development, Harris fought racial discrimination in the sale and rental of homes. She also tightened the department's control over the operations of the Federal National Mortgage Association. In 1979, she became secretary of health, education, and welfare (later changed to health and human services).

As secretary of health, education, and welfare, Harris issued new department guidelines that required federally funded colleges and universities to upgrade their sports programs for women.

Cyrus R. Vance is shown here with President Carter on 7 March 1977. (Courtesy Jimmy Carter Library.)

Cyrus R. Vance (1917–). Vance was appointed secretary of state by President Jimmy Carter in 1977. He had previously served as deputy defense secretary in the administration of Lyndon B. Johnson.

As secretary of state, Vance helped lay the groundwork for the Camp David Agreements (1979) between Egypt and Israel. He also participated in the Strategic Arms Limitation Talks (SALT) with the Soviet Union and supported passage of SALT II treaty. In 1980, Vance resigned because he opposed Carter's decision to launch the military attempt to free the U.S. hostages in Iran.

In 1995, Vance received the Harry S. Truman Award for Public Service.

FAMILY

CHRONOLOGICAL EVENTS

18 August 1927	(Eleanor) Rosalynn Smith born	12 April 1950	Son, James Earl (Chip), born
7 July 1946	Rosalynn Smith married Jimmy Carter	18 August 1952	Son, (Donnell) Jeffrey, born
		19 October 1967	Daughter, Amy Lynn, born
3 July 1947	Son, John William (Jack), born		

(Courtesy Library of Congress.)

(Bessie) Lillian Gordy Carter (1898–1983), President Carter's mother, was an extraordinary woman. She was known to everyone as Miss Lillian. Shortly after her husband's death in 1953, she took a job as housemother for a fraternity at Auburn University. She returned home after seven years.

She shocked everyone when she volunteered for the Peace Corps in 1966, at the age of 68. She was a registered nurse, and she was assigned to a clinic in India. The clinic was a 13-hour train ride from the airport in New Delhi.

Her letters from there were published as *Away From Home: Letters to my Family.* One of them read: "I didn't dream that in this remote corner of the world, so far away from the people and material things that I had always considered so necessary, I would discover what life is really all about. Sharing yourself with others, and accepting their love for you, is the most precious gift of all."

◄ Rosalynn Smith's best friend was Jimmy Carter's sister, Ruth, who later achieved fame as an evangelist. In First Lady From Plains, *she described falling in love with his picture even before they dated. She married him when she was 18 and he was 21, a new graduate of the United States Naval Academy, Annapolis.*

She helped him run his family business after he left the navy. She was the first First Lady since Eleanor Roosevelt to testify before Congress. She spoke on behalf of programs in mental health. (Courtesy Library of Congress.)

Amy Carter was born on 19 October 1967. At the time of her birth, her mother, Rosalynn, was 40 years old.

She received a bachelor of fine arts degree from Memphis College of Art, and she is currently pursuing a master's degree in art history. In 1995, she illustrated The Little Baby-Snoogle Fleejer, *a fairy tale which President Carter first told his children over 30 years ago.* (Courtesy Library of Congress.) ►

PLACES

JIMMY CARTER NATIONAL HISTORIC SITE

P.O. Box 392 • Plains, Georgia 31780 • Tel: (912) 824-3413

Located 50 miles southeast of Columbus. Can be reached via U.S. 280. The visitor center, located in the old railroad depot in downtown Plains, contains a small museum. Open daily from 9 A.M. to 5 P.M. Closed Christmas and New Year's Day. No admission fee. Handicapped accessible. The Carter boyhood home, and the Carter family home on Woodland Drive are both privately owned and not open to the public. The site contains the Carter boyhood home, the Plains railroad depot, the Plains High School, and the Carter family home. For more information, write: Superintendent, Andersonville National Historic Site, Route 1, Box 85, Andersonville, GA 31711. Administered by the National Park Service, U.S. Department of the Interior.

▲ *The Carter boyhood home, along with Jimmy Carter's present home on Woodland Drive, the Plains railroad depot, and the Plains High School, comprise the Jimmy Carter National Historic Site.*
(Courtesy Jimmy Carter National Historic Site.)

On 1 October 1924, Jimmy Carter was born at Wise Hospital in Plains, Georgia. Four years later, the Carter family moved two-and-a-half miles west of Plains to Archery—where his father, Earl, purchased a 360-acre farm on the old Preston-Americus Road (now called the Old Plains Highway). The future president lived there until 1942, when he enrolled at the Georgia Institute of Technology in Atlanta.

▲ *The home on Woodland Drive in Plains, Georgia became the residence of the Carter family in 1962, and remained in use as the family home through his terms as state senator, governor and president.*
(Courtesy Jimmy Carter National Historic Site.)

In 1943, he was appointed to the Naval Academy in Annapolis.

The boyhood home is a one-story bungalow with a screened-in porch. The four front rooms were originally heated by fireplaces; Jimmy Carter's bedroom, located at the northeast corner, had no heat. The home had no indoor plumbing or electricity until 1937. In 1949, when Jimmy Carter was in the navy, his family moved back to Plains.

The Carter family home on Woodland Drive was constructed in 1961. It is a one-story, brick, ranch-style home with light green trim, full-length windows, and a detached two-story garage with guest quarters on the second story. The house remains the home of Jimmy and Rosalynn Carter and is secured as a presidential compound, closely guarded by the Secret Service. This is the only home that the Carters have owned.

▲ *The Plains railroad depot was built in 1888. It was Carter's campaign headquarters in 1976, and it is now used as a visitor center.* (Courtesy Jimmy Carter National Historic Site.)

JIMMY CARTER LIBRARY

One Copenhill Avenue • Atlanta, Georgia 30307-1498 • Tel: (404) 331-0296

Located approximately 15 miles from Atlanta's Hartsfield International Airport. It is part of the Carter Presidential Center. Open Monday through Saturday from 9 A.M. to 4:45 P.M.; Sunday from 12 P.M. to 4:45 P.M. Closed Thanksgiving, Christmas, and New Year's Day. Admission fee for those 16 and older. For tour reservation, call: (404) 331-3942. Operated by the National Archives and Records Administration.

The construction of the Carter Presidential Center was funded entirely by private donations totaling 28 million dollars that were collected from individuals, foundations, and corporations. At the dedication ceremony on 1 October 1986, President Carter said: "I want the Carter Presidential Center to be a great resource for the people of Georgia, the Nation and the world and an expression of my gratitude for having been able to serve." (Courtesy Jimmy Carter Library; photographer: David Stanhope) ▶

The library houses Carter's presidential papers and other materials relating to his administration and career. The archives include 27 million pages of documents, 1.5 million photographs, and 40,000 objects. An interactive video display called the Town Meeting allows visitors to ask Jimmy Carter a variety of questions about his presidency and life.

The library is located at the Carter Presidential Center. The center, dedicated on 1 October 1986, consists of four interconnected buildings that house the offices of Jimmy and Rosalynn Carter, the Task Force for Child Survival and Global 2000, the Carter Center of Emory University, and the library.

Everett Raymond

Ronald Reagan

CHRONOLOGICAL EVENTS

6 February 1911	Born, Tampico, Illinois
7 June 1932	Graduated from Eureka College, Illinois; became a radio sports announcer
1937	Became a motion picture actor
1942–1945	Served in U.S. Army
1947 and 1959	Elected president of the Screen Actors Guild
1954–1962	Hosted television program "General Electric Theater"
1962–1965	Hosted television series "Death Valley Days"
1964	Made his last film, *The Killers*
8 November 1966	Elected governor of California
3 November 1970	Reelected governor of California
1976	Ran unsuccessfully for Republican presidential nomination
4 November 1980	Elected president
20 January 1981	Inaugurated president
30 March 1981	Assassination attempt
7 July 1981	Appointed the first woman (Sandra Day O'Connor) to the Supreme Court
25 August 1982	First U.S. troops arrive in Lebanon
20 April 1983	Signed Social Security Amendments
October 1983	Ordered the invasion of Grenada
6 November 1984	Reelected president
21 January 1985	Inaugurated president
November 1985	Held first summit meeting with Mikhail Gorbachev
April 1986	Authorized air strikes against Libya in retaliation for terrorist acts against Americans
22 October 1986	Signed Tax Reform Act
May–July 1987	Iran-contra affair hearings
8 December 1987	Signed Intermediate-Range Nuclear Forces (INF) Treaty
January 1989	Retired to Bel-Air, California
1990	Published memoirs, *An American Life: The Autobiography*

BIOGRAPHY

In the 1985 movie *Back to the Future*, the hero travels back in time to the 1950s, where he sees an advertisement for the movie *Cattle Queen of Montana*, starring Ronald Reagan. When the hero notes that one day Reagan will be president of the United States, another character responds sarcastically, "Who will be vice president—Jerry Lewis?" As unlikely as it might have seemed from the vantage point of the 1950s, Reagan was elected in 1980 as the nation's fortieth president in an impressive victory surpassed only by his record-making landslide reelection in 1984. While his credentials for office may have seemed a bit unorthodox—he is the only professional actor to occupy the White House—he proved to be one of the nation's most popular presidents. He left office in 1989 with a higher public opinion rating than any other modern president, and is the only president since Dwight D. Eisenhower to serve two full terms.

Ronald Reagan was born in Tampico, Illinois on 6 February 1911. When he was 9, his family moved to the nearby town of Dixon, where he attended public school before entering Eureka College, a small Disciples of Christ college outside Peoria, Illinois. After graduating from Eureka in

1932, Reagan secured a job as a sports announcer for a Davenport, Iowa radio station, which merged with a Des Moines station in mid-1933.

▲ Ronald Reagan's first job after graduating from college was as a sportscaster with radio station WOC in Davenport, Iowa. He was transferred to radio station WHO in Des Moines and became well known as the voice of Big Ten football and major league baseball. (Courtesy Ronald Reagan Library.)

During a 1937 trip to California to cover baseball spring training, Reagan secured a screen test at the Warner Brothers movie studio. Executives at the movie studio were impressed with what they saw and offered him an acting contract, which he quickly accepted. His first part was that of a radio announcer in *Love Is on the Air*, and over the next two and a half decades he went on to appear in more than 50 movies, including *Knute Rockne—All American*, *King's Row*, and *Bedtime for Bonzo*. During World War II, he was called to active duty in the U.S. Army. He was later transferred to the Army Air Force where he made training films. By the time he made his last movie, in 1964, he had become a television personality, as host for and occasional actor in both "The General Electric Theater" from 1954 to 1962 and "Death Valley Days" from 1962 to 1965.

Reagan's personal life centered on his acting career. He met his first wife, the actress Jane Wyman, on a film set in 1938. Married in 1940, they had one child, Maureen, and adopted another,

▲ Reagan worked as a life guard at Lowell Park on the Rock River, Illinois during the summers of 1926 to 1933. (Courtesy Ronald Reagan Library.)

Michael, before divorcing in 1949. In 1952, he married another aspiring actress, Nancy Davis, with whom he had two children, Patricia and Ronald. Although Nancy Reagan appeared in three television dramas in 1962, her last film role was in *Hellcats of the Navy* in 1957, the only movie she made with her husband.

Ronald Reagan's first move into politics came in 1947, when he was elected president of the Screen Actors Guild, an actors' union affiliated with the American Federation of Labor. He served six consecutive one-year terms in that capacity and was reelected in 1959. While he began his tenure as a liberal New Deal Democrat, he moved to the right in the early 1950s, taking a strong anti-communist position in response to congressional investigations in Hollywood. He campaigned as a Democrat for Dwight D. Eisenhower in 1952 and 1956 and for Richard M. Nixon in 1960. During that period, as a public relations representative for the General Electric Company, he toured the nation giving speeches praising the importance of free enterprise and warning of the dangers of big government. He completed his conversion from liberal to conservative by joining the Republican Party in 1962.

In 1964, the year he made his last movie, Reagan made his first splash in national politics with a television address in support of Barry Goldwater, the Republican presidential candidate. Goldwater lost, but a group of California businessmen was sufficiently impressed with Reagan to propose that he run for governor of the state. Although never having run for or held public office, Reagan proved a skillful campaigner, pulling ahead of five other candidates to win the 1966 Republican nomination for governor with 64.7 percent of the vote. In the general election, the Democratic incumbent did not take the actor-politician seriously, but Reagan proved an impressive vote-getter, defeating his opponent by nearly a million votes, the largest majority by which a sitting governor has been defeated in U.S. history.

Reagan served as governor of California for two four-year terms. Facing an unfriendly Democratic-controlled legislature for six of those years, he had limited success in carrying out the conservative agenda he supported in his campaigns. While he was in favor of cutting state expenditures and lowering taxes, the state budget more than doubled during his tenure. He sponsored three tax increases, one of which was the largest in state history. He also campaigned against welfare fraud but had to compromise with the state legislature, which agreed to tighten the eligibility requirements but also insisted on increasing benefits for those eligible. Opposed to the lenience of state university administrators toward student radicals, especially at University of California, Berkeley, Reagan cut funding for the state's higher education system. By the end of his tenure, he supported government spending at more than double the level when he came into office.

ELECTION OF 1976. Reagan decided not to run for a third term as governor in 1974. Instead, he made a bid for the 1976 Republican presidential nomination. He expected to run as Richard Nixon's successor but ended up challenging the incumbent Gerald R. Ford, who had become president upon Nixon's resignation in 1974. Reagan and his advisers hoped that, because primaries played an increasingly important role in the party's nominating process, Reagan's popularity with voters would give him the advantage. While he did indeed prove strong in the South and the West, Ford managed to secure the party's nomination, only to lose to the Democratic nominee, Jimmy Carter. Reagan immediately began planning and organizing for the 1980 election. Although Reagan did not formally announce his candidacy until November 1979, a Reagan-backed political action committee provided financial support for candidates in 1978 congressional elections, thereby establishing an important support base for his candidacy in 1980.

ELECTION OF 1980. Reagan's bid stumbled at first with an unimaginative effort that cost him the Iowa caucuses. He quickly rebounded to win the New Hampshire primary in early 1980 and eventually won all but four of the primaries held that year. He also proved more popular with other

Ronald Reagan won 44 states and received 489 electoral votes. Jimmy Carter received 49 electoral votes and Independent candidate John Anderson received no electoral votes although he did receive 7 percent of the popular vote. President Reagan was sworn in on 20 January 1981. Chief Justice Warren Burger administered the oath. (Courtesy Ronald Reagan Library.)

state caucuses, winning 400 out of 478 delegate votes. By the time the Republicans assembled in Detroit for their convention, the nomination was his. He chose as his running mate George Bush, a former Texas congressman and a rival for the presidential nomination.

The campaigns of both Reagan and the incumbent Carter generated little enthusiasm among voters. Reagan blamed Carter for the nation's mounting economic problems and promised to slow inflation and lower unemployment with a package of proposals that included a 30 percent cut in taxes and a balanced budget. He also decried the United States's loss of leadership in international affairs and, in the best cold war rhetoric, pledged to rebuild the nation's defenses.

But perhaps more important than the issues were the differences in style between the two candidates: the ever-charming Reagan conveyed a sense of optimism and hope, while Carter, stiff and ineffective, talked of limits and a national crisis of confidence. Nevertheless, the race proved hard to predict. While Reagan lost his initial 15 percent lead in the polls, and the two candidates appeared even by Election Day, Reagan won by a landslide, sweeping all but six states and the District of Columbia. Moreover, the Republicans gained control of the U.S. Senate for the first time in 26 years.

Reagan promised to be a different kind of president, bringing Hollywood glamor to Washington and reveling in the pageantry of the White House and the trappings of the presidency that his more populist predecessor had avoided. After four years of a president who seemed more and more weighted down by the burdens of office, the public enjoyed Reagan's optimism and self-confidence, especially in the face of an assassination attempt in March 1981 and colon cancer surgery in 1985.

But while Reagan was often ridiculed as "the great entertainer," as all style and no substance, he took office with a very clearly expressed agenda: to rebuild the economy through tax cuts, deregulation, and domestic budget cuts; to pursue a social agenda that included constitutional amendments to prohibit abortion and to restore prayer in public schools; and to rebuild the nation's military strength and replace the policy of détente (easing of tensions) with a hard line assertion of U.S. opposition to communist aggression. He proved most successful with the first—domestic economy policy.

DOMESTIC POLICY. The key to the Reagan administration's arguments for both tax cuts and a balanced budget was supply-side economics, which proposed to resolve the nation's economic

President and Mrs. Reagan loved the glamor and pageantry of the presidency. In 1985, they received Prince Charles and Princess Diana at the White House. The Royal couple were visiting Washington as patrons of the National Gallery Exhibition, "Treasure Houses of Britain." (Courtesy Ronald Reagan Library.)

FIRST INAUGURAL ADDRESS

. . . So, as we begin, let us take inventory. We are a nation that has a government—not the other way around. And this makes us special among the nations of the earth. Our government has no power except that granted it by the people. It is time to check and reverse the growth of government which shows signs of having grown beyond the consent of the governed.

It is my intention to curb the size and influence of the federal establishment and to demand recognition of the distinction between the powers granted to the federal government and those reserved to the states or to the people. All of us need to be reminded that the federal government did not create the states; the states created the federal government.

Now, so there will be no misunderstanding, it is not my intention to do away with government. It is, rather, to make it work—work with us, not over us; to stand by our side, not ride on our back. Government can and must provide opportunity, not smother it; foster productivity, not stifle it. . . .

• *Reagan delivered these remarks at his first Inauguration on 20 January 1981.*

problems without the pain of a recession. According to this theory, called "Reaganomics" by the media, the old solutions—cutting government spending to curb inflation; increasing spending to address unemployment—did not work any longer since the nation faced both problems at once. Instead, the Reaganites proposed to generate economic growth by stimulating business activity with tax cuts and other incentives (including weakening environmental and safety regulations) that would promote the savings and investment needed for expanding production and increasing jobs. The growing economy would, in turn, generate increased tax revenues, which, along with cuts and new priorities in federal spending, would make it possible to balance the budget and slow inflation.

This was Reagan's agenda when he assumed office in 1981, and he moved quickly to secure a 25 percent tax cut for individuals and faster corporate tax write-offs—the largest income tax cut in U.S. history—and to cut the federal budget by $39 billion. But the economy did not respond as predicted. The supply-side stimulants did not generate growth, and the nation slipped by mid-1981 into the deepest recession since the Depression. Companies went bankrupt and unemployment increased by the end of 1982 to 10.7 percent, the highest level since 1941. Yet despite cuts in Social Security, medical aid, and other "safety net" programs for the poor and the unemployed, the federal deficit grew. Tax revenues fell short of estimates and increased defense expenditures offset cuts in social programs. Meanwhile, increased borrowing abroad to cover the deficit pushed interest rates and the value of the dollar up, increasing the trade deficit, undermining the competitiveness of U.S. businesses, and deepening the recession.

A tax increase in 1982—the largest in history—had little impact on the growing deficit, which hit record levels in 1982 and again in 1983. By 1983, however, the economy was beginning to recover, and by 1984, when Reagan was up for reelection, the economy was strong and inflation low, despite the still rising deficit. While the Democrats had picked up seats in the House in 1982, the revived economy in 1984 ensured the reelection of the Reagan-Bush ticket. Reagan won by an even wider margin than in 1980, taking every state but Minnesota (the home state of Walter F. Mondale, his Democratic opponent) and the District of Columbia and securing 525 electoral votes, the highest number ever won by a presidential candidate.

In his second term, Reagan focused on tax reform. In 1986, he secured congressional approval of a reform package that included sim-

SECOND INAUGURAL ADDRESS

. . . Four years ago, I spoke to you of a new beginning and we have accomplished that. But in another sense, our new beginning is a continuation of that beginning created two centuries ago when, for the first time in history, government, the people said, was not our master, it is our servant; its only power that which we the people allow it to have.

That system has never failed us, but, for a time, we failed the system. We asked things of government that government was not equipped to give. We yielded authority to the national government that properly belonged to states or to local governments or to the people themselves. We allowed taxes and inflation to rob us of our earnings and savings and watched the great industrial machine that had made us the most productive people on earth slow down and the number of unemployed increase. . . .

A dynamic economy, with more citizens working and paying taxes, will be our strongest tool to bring down budget deficits. But an almost unbroken fifty years of deficit spending has finally brought us to a time of reckoning. We have come to a turning point, a moment for hard decisions. I have asked the Cabinet and my staff a question, and now I put the same question to all of you: If not us, who? And if not now, when? It must be done by all of us going forward with a program aimed at reaching a balanced budget. We can then begin reducing the national debt.

I will shortly submit a budget to the Congress aimed at freezing government program spending for the next year. Beyond that, we must take further steps to permanently control government's power to tax and spend. We must act now to protect future generations from government's desire to spend its citizens' money and tax them into servitude when the bills come due. Let us make it unconstitutional for the federal government to spend more than the federal government takes in. . . .

• *President Reagan delivered his second Inaugural Address on 21 January 1985. He again called for less government and expressed his concern over a balanced budget. During his term in office, the national debt tripled.*

plification of the tax system and elimination of many special tax preferences and deductions. As the economy continued to thrive, the federal deficit actually declined in 1987, the first time during Reagan's tenure. But it still exceeded any of the deficits incurred by previous administrations. Indeed, during Reagan's term in office, the national debt tripled, and the trade deficit increased fourfold, making the United States a debtor nation. Reagan never admitted responsibility for those problems but focused instead on his administration's engineering of what turned out to be the longest peacetime boom in history. By the time he left office, unemployment had

dropped to 5.5 percent, and inflation was down to between 4 and 6 percent from a peak of more than 15 percent during the Carter administration.

While Reagan could claim some success with his economic policies, he accomplished far less of the social portion of his domestic program. The administration's conservative social agenda was perhaps most clearly reflected in its policies regarding minorities. Under Reagan, the Justice Department supported legal challenges to court-ordered school busing and cut back on enforcement of antidiscrimination and fair housing legislation. Furthermore, Reagan virtually destroyed the Commission on Civil Rights and in

John W. Hinckley, Jr. attempted to assassinate President Reagan on 30 March 1981 as he walked out of the Washington Hilton. One of Hinckley's bullets lodged only an inch from the President's heart. (Courtesy Ronald Reagan Library.)

1988 vetoed a major civil rights bill, only to be overridden by Congress. His record was better, however, in regard to women. He appointed the first woman to the Supreme Court, Sandra Day O'Connor, and was the first president to have three women serving in cabinet-level positions at once. Other "social agenda" items that the Reagan White House supported were drug testing of employees and control of allegedly obscene films and publications. But while his call for return to an older morality ensured him the support of right-to-life groups and Christian fundamentalists, he took little direct action on either abortion or prayer in public schools. Instead, Reagan focused his attention on establishing a more conservative core in the Supreme Court, which would in any case be the final arbiter on those issues. He was successful in 1986 in securing Senate approval of

the appointments of Justice William Rehnquist, the most conservative member of the Court at the time, as chief justice and of the conservative judge Antonin Scalia as an associate justice. But in 1987, with the Democrats back in control of the Senate, he lost a bitter fight over the appointment of a hard-line conservative, Robert H. Bork. After the Bork defeat, Reagan nominated another conservative, Douglas H. Ginsburg. Ginsburg withdrew when a controversy arose over his past use of marijuana. On his third try, however, he was more successful. He won the appointment of Anthony Kennedy, a less controversial and more mainstream conservative jurist.

FOREIGN POLICY. Reagan changed the tone but did not really change the direction of U.S. foreign policy, despite his criticism of his predecessors' détente policies and his insistence that the buildup of the Soviet Union's arms and the United States's neglect of its defense meant that the latter faced a "window of vulnerability" to nuclear attack. He used the vulnerability argument to secure increased defense expenditures, even when the consequence was a growing deficit. Reagan was particularly insistent on the necessity of the Strategic Defense Initiative (SDI), a space-based missile system. Critics called SDI "Star Wars" and argued it was both too expensive and technically unworkable.

The Reagan-sponsored defense buildup reflected a return to cold war assumptions and a deemphasis on détente with the Soviet Union. While President Carter had focused on human rights issues, Reagan was more concerned about controlling the expansionist and interventionist policies that he attributed to the Soviet "evil empire." Tensions increased between the two nations after the Soviets shot down a South Korean airliner in 1983 and the United States deployed intermediate-range missiles in Western Europe. However, relations improved during Reagan's second term through a series of summit meetings that reached a climax in a nuclear arms reduction agreement.

While there was no direct military engagement of the United States and the Soviets, Reagan did use military action as an instrument of his anti-communist foreign policy and as a deterrent to terrorism. The best example of the former was the invasion of the Caribbean island of Grenada in October 1983. Reagan claimed that U.S. intervention was necessary to subdue a rebel coup, protect Americans in Grenada, and stop Soviet and Cuban influence. While Reagan enjoyed considerable popular support for this swift and decisive engagement, he found success more difficult to achieve when dealing with terrorists and the Middle East. Terrorist acts that involved Americans included a 1983 bombing in Beirut that killed 241 U.S. soldiers; the highjacking of TWA flight 847 in June 1985; the highjacking of the Italian ocean liner *Achille Lauro* in October 1985; bombings of air-

ports in Rome and Vienna at the end of that year; and the bombing of a West German nightclub in April 1986. The Reagan administration's antiterrorism policies culminated in air strikes in 1986 against Libya, a nation viewed by the White House as the primary instigator.

The Reagan White House also provided aid, including arms and military advisers, to conservative forces battling leftist regimes and rebels in various locations around the world, including Afghanistan, Angola, El Salvador, and Nicaragua. Reagan was willing to support even a right-wing dictatorship so long as it was anti-communist. This policy proved most questionable in Nicaragua, where the United States proposed to assist anti-communist guerrillas, known as the contras, against the leftist Sandinista government. The determination of the Reagan administration to help the contras despite congressional opposition led to the Iran-contra affair, which came to dominate the last two years of Reagan's tenure. The story unfolded bit by bit in late 1986 and 1987. Basically, the Reagan administration secretly sold arms to Iran in the hope of securing the release of hostages held by the Lebanese and then diverted some of the profits from the arms sale to the contras in Nicaragua, despite a U.S. policy that forbade arms sales to nations that supported terrorism and a congressional ban on military aid to the contras. Reagan claimed that his advisers had not fully informed him of what was going on and that his national security adviser Vice Admiral John Poindexter and Poindexter's aide Lieutenant Colonel Oliver North had acted without his knowledge or approval. A presidential commission established to investigate the matter found Reagan confused and uninformed, lacking control over his own aides. A joint congressional committee conducted its own hearings and concluded in November 1987 that the President should be held responsible for failing to ensure that the nation's laws were upheld, although it was Poindexter, North, and others who were subsequently indicted and tried for their involvement.

(above) President Reagan met with Mikhail Gorbachev several times. In December 1987, they signed the Intermediate-Range Nuclear Forces (INF) Treaty , a major arms-control agreement. *(below)* One year later, the Gorbachevs visited the White House. (Courtesy Ronald Reagan Library.)

British Prime Minister Margaret Thatcher was Reagan's firmest friend and ally.
"The two conservative world leaders often reinforced one another at international gatherings, and Thatcher gave Reagan high marks for speaking out early and often against Soviet adventurism and Marxist ideology . . . Thatcher said in a tribute late in the Reagan presidency, 'From a strong fortress of his convictions, he set out to enlarge freedom the world over at a time when freedom was in retreat—and he succeeded.'" Lou Cannon, "Reagan, Ronald," in Encyclopedia of the American Presidency, *edited by Leonard W. Levy and Louis Fisher.* (Courtesy Ronald Reagan Library.)

The Iran-contra affair focused public attention on Reagan's hands-off management style and undermined his reputation for honesty and commitment to principle. Nevertheless, he remained one of the nation's most popular presidents. Indeed, critics called him the "Teflon president" on whom nothing would stick. If he appeared at times to be vague on facts or poorly informed on issues, he still won the people's support with a simple and reassuring message of optimism and self-confidence about the nation's future.

After the inauguration in January 1989 of George Bush as the forty-first president, Reagan and his wife returned to California, where they wrote their memoirs, joined the lecture circuit, and moved forward with plans for the Reagan Library.

President and Mrs. Reagan retired to their 688-acre estate north of Santa Barbara, California. (Courtesy Ronald Reagan Library.)

VICE PRESIDENT

George Herbert Walker Bush
(1924–)

CHRONOLOGICAL EVENTS

1924	Born, Milton, Massachusetts, 12 June
1942	Enlisted in the U.S. Navy
1948	Graduated from Yale University, Connecticut
1966	Elected to U.S. House of Representatives
1970	Appointed U.S. ambassador to the United Nations
1974	Appointed liaison officer to the People's Republic of China
1975	Appointed director of the Central Intelligence Agency
1980	Elected vice president
1988	Elected president
1992	Ran unsuccessfully for reelection as president

BIOGRAPHY

The son of a U.S. senator, George Bush grew up in suburban Connecticut. Graduating from Phillips Academy, he enlisted as a navy pilot during World War II. Shot down and rescued at sea, he received the navy's Distinguished Flying Cross.

Bush returned to marry Barbara Pierce, attend Yale University, and become a Texas oil company executive. He lost a race for the U.S. Senate in 1964, but two years later, won election to the U.S. House of Representatives. President Richard Nixon persuaded Bush to run for the Senate again in 1970, but he lost to the Democrat Lloyd Bentsen.

Nixon appointed Bush ambassador to the United Nations. Bush later headed the Republican National Committee during the investigations of the Watergate scandal. When secret tapes revealed that the President had participated in a coverup, Bush urged Nixon to resign.

Under President Gerald Ford, Bush represented the United States in China and became director of the Central Intelligence Agency. After Ford was defeated, Bush announced that he would be a candidate for president in 1980. Although he won the Iowa caucuses, he lost the nomination to former California Governor Ronald Reagan, whom he had accused of advocating "voodoo economics." After efforts to nominate Ford for vice president failed, Reagan chose Bush. They defeated the incumbent, President Jimmy Carter.

Learning from his years in appointed office, Bush deferred to President Reagan on all matters. He devoted his attention to chairing task forces on federal deregulation, on reducing bureaucratic red tape, and on drug smuggling. Renominated in 1984, Bush debated New York Representative Geraldine Ferraro, the first woman candidate for vice president, on television.

During Reagan's second term, the Iran-contra scandal raised questions about the Vice President's involvement, but Bush insisted that he had been "out of the loop." In 1988, he won the Republican presidential nomination, selecting Indiana Senator Dan Quayle as his running mate. Their campaign against the Democratic candidates, Michael Dukakis and Lloyd Bentsen, featured negative advertising and Bush's pledge never to raise taxes. Bush became the first sitting vice president in 156 years to win the presidency on his own.

THE CABINET

SECRETARY OF STATE
Alexander M. Haig, Jr., 1981
George P. Shultz, 1982, 1985

SECRETARY OF THE TREASURY
Donald T. Regan, 1981
James A. Baker, III, 1985
Nicholas F. Brady, 1988

ATTORNEY GENERAL
William French Smith, 1981
Edwin Meese, III, 1985
Richard Thornburgh, 1988

SECRETARY OF THE INTERIOR
James G. Watt, 1981
William P. Clark, 1983
Donald P. Hodel, 1985

SECRETARY OF AGRICULTURE
John R. Block, 1981, 1985
Richard E. Lyng, 1986

SECRETARY OF COMMERCE
Malcolm Baldrige, 1981, 1985
C. William Verity, Jr., 1987

George P. Shultz (1920–). Shultz was appointed secretary of state by President Ronald Reagan in 1982. He had previously served as secretary of labor and secretary of the treasury in the administration of Richard M. Nixon.

As secretary of state, Shultz advocated a strong U.S. presence in the Middle East and supported the use of force against terrorism. He opposed the plan of National Security Advisors Robert McFarlane and John Poindexter to sell military arms to Iran in exchange for the release of U.S. hostages in Lebanon.

In 1987, he helped negotiate the Intermediate-Range Nuclear Forces (INF) Treaty with the Soviet Union.

George P. Shultz is shown here with President Reagan at the Annenberg Estate in Palm Springs, California.
(Courtesy Ronald Reagan Library.)

THE CABINET

SECRETARY OF LABOR
Raymond J. Donovan, 1981
William E. Brock, III, 1985
Ann D. McLaughlin, 1987

SECRETARY OF DEFENSE
Caspar Weinberger, 1981, 1985
Frank Carlucci, 1987

SECRETARY OF HOUSING AND URBAN DEVELOPMENT
Samuel R. Pierce, Jr., 1981, 1985

SECRETARY OF TRANSPORTATION
Andrew L. Lewis, 1981
Elizabeth H. Dole, 1983
James H. Burnley, IV, 1987

SECRETARY OF ENERGY
James B. Edwards, 1981
Donald P. Hodel, 1983
John S. Herrington, 1985

SECRETARY OF HEALTH AND HUMAN SERVICES
Richard S. Schweiker, 1981
Margaret M. Heckler, 1983, 1985
Otis R. Bowen, 1985

SECRETARY OF EDUCATION
Terrel H. Bell, 1981
William J. Bennett, 1985
Lauro F. Cavazos, 1988

Richard Thornburgh is shown here with President Reagan in the Press Briefing Room. The President was announcing Thornburgh's nomination as attorney general. (Courtesy Ronald Reagan Library.)

Richard Thornburgh (1932–). Thornburgh was appointed attorney general by President Ronald Reagan in 1988. He had previously served as governor of Pennsylvania (1978–1986). In 1979, he gained national attention for his leadership during the Three Mile Island nuclear power plant accident.

As attorney general, Thornburgh became heavily involved in President Reagan's "war on drugs." Thornburgh pledged to support "a vigorous effort to make drug trafficking and drug abuse public enemy number one."

Thornburgh was reappointed by President George Bush in 1989. During his tenure, he argued for the restriction of abortion rights. He also secured increased funding for law enforcement. In 1991, he resigned to run, unsuccessfully, for the U.S. Senate.

FAMILY

CHRONOLOGICAL EVENTS

4 January 1914	Jane Wyman (Sarah Jane Fulks) born	18 July 1949	Jane Wyman divorced Ronald Reagan
6 July 1923	Nancy Davis (Anne Francis Robbins) born	4 March 1952	Nancy Davis married Ronald Reagan
26 January 1940	Jane Wyman married Ronald Reagan	21 October 1952	Daughter, Patricia (Patti) (Reagan) Davis, born
4 January 1941	Daughter, Maureen, born	20 May 1958	Son, Ronald (Ron) Prescott, born
18 March 1945	Son, Michael, born		

The 1981 Inaugural Family Photo shows, from left to right: Mrs. Reagan's nephew and niece, Geoffrey Davis and Anne Davis; Dennis Revell (Maureen's husband); Maureen Reagan; Michael Reagan holding son, Cameron; Michael's wife, Colleen; President and Mrs. Reagan; Bess Reagan (Neil's wife); the President's brother, Neil; Patricia Davis (Richard's wife); Mrs. Reagan's brother, Richard Davis; Patti Reagan Davis; Doria (Ron's wife); and Ron, Jr. (Courtesy Ronald Reagan Library.)

(Courtesy Ronald Reagan Library.)

Nancy Davis Reagan was born Anne Francis Robbins. She was adopted by her mother's second husband, Dr. Loyal Davis. She majored in drama at Smith College and became an actress after graduation in 1943. She married Reagan in 1952, and they had two children.

Patti left college and has had many minor acting jobs. She has been an outspoken critic of her parents, but she became friendly with the family again when her father's Alzheimer's disease became known. Her first novel, *Home Front* (with Maureen Strange Foster, 1986), was a best-seller.

Ron left Yale University after one year to study ballet. He later left the Joffrey Ballet. In 1985, he became an entertainment reporter for *Good Morning America*.

President Reagan had a daughter, Maureen, with his first wife, Jane Wyman, and they adopted a son, Michael. In 1982, Maureen lost the Republican nomination in California for the U.S. Senate. In 1984, she campaigned for her father's reelection. She wrote a book, *First Father, First Daughter* (1989).

Michael became a professional speedboat racer. He was not close to the family. He wrote of the problems he had as a child in *On the Outside Looking In* (with Joe Hyams, 1988).

PLACES

RONALD REAGAN BIRTHPLACE

111 Main Street • Tampico, Illinois 61283 • (815) 438-2815

Located approximately 58 miles southwest of Rockford. Can be reached via I-88 at the Sterling Rock Falls exit. Take Illinois Route 88 South to Route 172 West, then turn south onto Route 172. Open by appointment only. Donations requested. Museum and gift shop located on first floor. Birthplace apartment not handicapped accessible. Administered by Paul and Helen Nicely.

In 1906, Ronald Reagan's parents, John and Nelle, came to Tampico, Illinois, to open a dry-goods store. They rented a six-room apartment on the second floor of The First National Bank of Tampico. On 6 February 1911, their second son, Ronald Wilson, was born there. In May 1911, the Reagans moved to a house on Glassburn Street in Tampico. They then moved to Chicago in December 1914 and continued to move from town to town throughout his childhood.

The birthplace is maintained by Paul and Helen Nicely, who have assembled a collection of period furnishings and mementos from Ronald Reagan's entertainment and political careers. A museum and a gift shop are located on the first floor.

RONALD REAGAN BOYHOOD HOME

816 South Hennepin Avenue • Dixon, Illinois 61021
Tel: (815) 288-3404

Located 40 miles southwest of Rockford. Take Route 30 West to Route 88 West into Dixon. Open December, January, and February, on Saturday from 10 A.M. to 5 P.M. and Sunday from 1 A.M. to 4 P.M.; March through November, Monday to Saturday except Tuesday, from 10 A.M. to 4 P.M. Closed Christmas, Thanksgiving, New Year's Day, and Easter. No admission fee; donations welcome. Guided tours available. Group tours available by advance reservation. Reception center and restrooms are handicapped accessible. The boyhood home is not handicapped accessible, but a video tour of the site is provided. Gift shop. Administered by the Ronald Reagan Home Preservation Foundation.

On 6 December 1920, when Ronald Reagan was nine, his family moved to Dixon, Illinois. They moved into a two-story house located at 816 South Hennepin Avenue that was originally owned by Reverend John Dixon, the founder of Dixon. Four years later, the Reagans moved to 338 Everett Street in Dixon.

The boyhood home, built in 1891, contains furniture similar to that which was in the house when the Reagans lived there. On President Reagan's birthday, 6 February 1984, he visited the site with his wife, Nancy, and his brother, Neil. (Courtesy Ronald Reagan Library.)

RANCHO DEL CIELO

Santa Barbara County, California

> *Located approximately 12 miles north of Santa Barbara, in the Santa Ynez Mountains. It is not open to the public.*

▲ *Rancho del Cielo — Spanish for ranch in the sky — is the home of former President Reagan and his wife, Nancy.* (Courtesy Ronald Reagan Library.)

The Reagans purchased the property for $526,600 in 1974. The two-bedroom, 100-year-old ranch house is situated on 688 acres of land, 2,200 feet above the Pacific Ocean. Also located on the property is a small stable for horses and a 100-foot-long, man-made pond. The property is closed to the public and closely guarded by the Secret Service. Mrs. Reagan put the property up for sale in the summer of 1996.

RONALD REAGAN LIBRARY

40 Presidential Drive • Simi Valley, California 93065 • Tel: (805) 522-8444

> *Located off State Highway 23, exit east onto Olsen Road, approximately 30 miles northwest of Los Angeles. The museum is open Monday through Saturday from 10 A.M. to 5 P.M. and Sunday from 12 P.M. to 5 P.M. The research room is open Monday through Friday from 9 A.M. to 4:30 P.M. Closed Thanksgiving, Christmas, and New Year's Day. Admission fee for museum. Children ages 15 and under admitted free. Groups of 20 or more should make advance reservations. Operated and maintained by the National Archives and Records Administration.*

The library houses approximately 50 million pages of documents, including records created or received by the President and White House staff members, 1.5 million still photographs, and more than 75,000 gifts. The site is situated on 29 acres of land on a 100-acre tract in Ventura County, California. President Bush and former Presidents Reagan, Carter, Ford, and Nixon attended the dedication ceremonies on 4 November 1991. The library was opened for research on 12 November 1991.

◄ *At the dedication ceremony, Ronald Reagan stated: "The doors of this library are open now and all are welcome. The judgment of history is left to you — the people. I have no fears of that, for we have done our best. And so I say, come and learn from it."* (Courtesy Ronald Reagan Library; photographer: Wendy Sparks.)

George Bush

41ST PRESIDENT OF THE UNITED STATES OF AMERICA

CHRONOLOGICAL EVENTS

12 June 1924	Born, Milton, Massachusetts
1942	Enlisted in the U.S. Navy
1943	Became youngest pilot in the U.S. Navy
1945	Discharged from U.S. Navy; enrolled at Yale University
21 June 1948	Graduated from Yale University, Connecticut
1948	Moved to Texas to work in oil business
1964	Ran unsuccessfully for U.S. Senate
8 November 1966	Elected to U.S. House of Representatives
5 November 1968	Reelected to U.S. House of Representatives
1970	Ran unsuccessfully for U.S. Senate
11 December 1970	Appointed U.S. ambassador to United Nations
19 January 1973	Appointed chairman of the Republican National Committee
September 1974	Appointed chief of U.S. Liaison office in Beijing, China
December 1975	Appointed director of Central Intelligence Agency (CIA)
1977	Resigned from CIA; returned to Texas
4 November 1980	Elected vice president
6 November 1984	Reelected vice president
8 November 1988	Elected president
20 January 1989	Inaugurated president
20 December 1989	Ordered Operation Just Cause, U.S. invasion of Panama to capture General Manuel Noriega
19 November 1990	Signed Treaty on Conventional Armed Forces in Europe
26 June 1990	Released written statement supporting the second largest tax increase in U.S. history
2 August 1990	Saddam Hussein's Iraqi forces invade Kuwait
26 July 1990	Signed Americans with Disabilities Act
17 January 1991	Launched military offensive, Operation Desert Storm, in the Persian Gulf
31 July 1992	Signed Strategic Arms Reduction Treaty (START)
30 November 1992	Defeated for reelection as president
4 December 1992	Announced dispatch of U.S. troops to Somalia
20 January 1993	Retired to Houston, Texas

BIOGRAPHY

With his election in 1988 as the forty-first president of the United States, George Bush became the fourteenth vice president to assume the higher office. The most distinctive thing about his route to office, however, was his record of service in three presidential administrations: Richard Nixon appointed him the U.S. delegate to the United Nations, Gerald Ford appointed him chief of the U.S. Liaison Office in China and then director of the Central Intelligence Agency, and Ronald Reagan chose him as his running mate. Reagan delegated significant responsibilities to him during his two terms in office. To find a similar executive branch veteran, one would have to go back to William Howard Taft, who took office eight decades before and similarly served only one term as president.

George Bush enlisted in the U.S. Navy on his 18th birthday. This picture was taken during his primary flight training at Minneapolis, Minnesota in 1942. (Courtesy The White House.)

George Bush was born in Milton, Massachusetts on 12 June 1924 but grew up in Connecticut. His father was a wealthy Wall Street investment banker and served as a U.S. senator from Connecticut from 1952 to 1963. The younger Bush attended exclusive private schools in New England and had planned to enter Yale University in 1942. With the U.S. entry into World War II, he postponed his plans and enlisted in the U.S. Navy. When commissioned in 1943, he was the navy's youngest pilot. Stationed in the Pacific, Bush flew 58 combat missions. One of these misions ended with the dramatic sea rescue of the young pilot after his bomber was downed by the Japanese. Two weeks after his return to the United States in late 1944, he married Barbara Pierce, a young woman from nearby Rye, New York, whom he had met the Christmas before his enlistment. Their first son, George, was born the following year. Over the next decade and a half, the Bushes had three more sons (John, Neil, and Marvin) and two daughters (Dorothy and Robin, who died of leukemia at the age of three).

After his discharge from the navy, Bush enrolled at Yale as originally planned. He captained the baseball team, was tapped for membership in Skull and Bones, the university's most exclusive secret society, and, in just three years, graduated Phi Beta Kappa with a B.A. in economics. Instead of going to work in his father's firm, Bush and his young family moved to Texas, where family connections provided him with entry into the oil business. In 1954, he cofounded the Zapata Offshore Company, which specialized in offshore drilling equipment, and served as its president until 1964, when his interests turned to politics.

Richard Nixon (right) appointed George Bush ambassador to the United Nations in 1971. President Nixon later asked Bush to become chairman of the Republican Party. Bush remained loyal to Nixon through the Watergate affair until the White House tapes were released. (Courtesy The Richard Nixon Library & Museum.)

EARLY POLITICAL CAREER. Despite its marginal role in Texas politics at the time, Bush cast his lot with the Republican Party. In 1962, he won election as the chair of the Republican Party's organization in Houston. Two years later, he launched a statewide campaign for the U.S. Senate seat held by the Democrat Ralph Yarborough. Bush won the Republican primary but lost to the incumbent in the general election. In 1966, he set his sights on a more realistic goal and became the first Republican to represent Houston in Congress. While he won conservative support for his opposition to the public accommodations provision of the 1964 Civil Rights Act, his overall record was more moderate and included support for open-housing legislation and birth-control programs.

Reelected to the House in 1968, Bush decided to make another try for the Senate in 1970, again winning the Republican nomination but losing to his Democratic opponent. Feeling an obligation to Bush because he had encouraged him to run, President Nixon appointed him as the Permanent Representative of the United States to the United Nations (UN). Despite his lack of foreign policy experience, the Senate unanimously confirmed him in 1971. Perhaps the most significant issue during his time at the UN was the fate of the Republic of China (Taiwan). Not informed by Nixon of secret U.S. efforts to establish diplomatic relations with the People's Republic of China, Bush argued unsuccessfully for allowing the Taiwan government to retain its seat in the General Assembly. Nevertheless, Bush remained loyal to Nixon and agreed in 1973 to take over as chair of the Republican National Committee, just as the full story of the Watergate break-ins began to emerge.

President Gerald Ford appointed Bush director of the Central Intelligence Agency (CIA). On 17 June 1976, Bush briefed Ford (standing, right) and other members of the National Security Council. He was pointing out safe escape routes for Americans from Beirut, Lebanon. (Courtesy Gerald R. Ford Library.)

Convinced that the President had not been involved in the break-in or in the attempted cover-up, Bush loyally defended Nixon until early August 1974, when the release of White House tape recordings revealed the extent of the President's involvement.

With Nixon's resignation, Gerald Ford became president and, in recognition of Bush's loyal service to the Republican Party, he offered him whatever assignment he wished. Bush chose to head the newly established U.S. Liaison Office in China, but Ford recalled him in 1975 to take over as director of the Central Intelligence Agency (CIA). The CIA was then in trouble with Congress because of revelations of past abuses of power and involvement in covert operations. During his year at the CIA, Bush blunted criticism, improved agency management, and raised staff morale. He left the CIA, however, after Ford's defeat by Jimmy Carter in the 1976 presidential election.

ELECTION OF 1980. Bush returned to Texas and resumed his business career, joining several corporations as a board director and consultant, but politics remained his real interest. Never one to set his sights low, he announced in May 1979 his intention to run for the Republican presidential nomination. In contrast to the harsh conservatism of the popular Ronald Reagan, Bush called for

Ronald Reagan chose George Bush to be his running mate. They easily defeated Jimmy Carter and Walter Mondale in 1980 and Walter Mondale and Geraldine Ferraro in 1984. They met in the office of former President Reagan in California on 1 March 1990. (Courtesy Bush Presidential Materials Project.)

moderation and labeled as "voodoo economics" the Californian's plan to cut taxes, increase military spending, and still balance the budget. He started off strong, winning the Iowa caucus, but soon fell behind in the primary battles for delegate votes. After he lost the Texas primary, Bush yielded to Reagan and withdrew from the race. After his nomination, Reagan asked Bush to be his running mate, despite Bush's outspoken criticism of him in the primary races. In the campaign that followed, Bush loyally minimized their differences and adopted Reagan's conservative agenda. Reagan and Bush proved impressive vote-getters, winning 44 states to win the White House in 1980 and 49 states when they ran for reelection in 1984.

Reagan gave his vice president significant responsibilities. Bush chaired the National Security Council's crisis management team and headed task forces on crime, terrorism, and drug smuggling. He also chaired a task force concerning government control of businesses. The last yielded doubtful results—airline deregulation led to bankruptcies, mergers, and higher prices. The deregulation of savings and loan associations opened the way to abuses that ultimately cost taxpayers $500 billion. As vice president, Bush also filled in for Reagan when he was temporarily disabled after an assassination attempt in 1981 and by colon cancer surgery in 1985. Despite this, Bush claimed that he was "out of the loop" when the administration admitted in late 1986 to secretly selling arms to Iran in exchange for the

George Bush surprised the Republican National Convention in New Orleans in 1988 when he chose as his running mate J. Danforth Quayle, a young and relatively unknown senator from Indiana. They easily defeated the Democratic nominees, Michael Dukakis and Lloyd Bentsen. Bush and Quayle are shown in the Oval Office in 1989. (Courtesy Bush Presidential Materials Project.)

release of U.S. hostages held in the Middle East and then using the profits to support anti-communist guerrillas in Nicaragua. Bush denied any knowledge of these illegal activities despite the involvement of his aides and his own participation in several key meetings. The specifics of Bush's tenure as vice president were less important, however, than his demonstration that he was a team player loyal to the President and thus Reagan's rightful political successor.

1988 ELECTION YEAR. In October 1987, Bush staked his claim as Reagan's heir and announced his intention to run for the presidency. He lost the Iowa caucuses, but subsequent wins in the New Hampshire primary and in Southern primaries put him far ahead of his challengers. He won the nomination on the first ballot at the Republican Party's August convention and chose as his running mate J. Danforth Quayle, a young and relatively unknown senator from Indiana. On the campaign trail, Bush was determined to rally loyal Reaganites and accordingly promised that his administration would continue the domestic and foreign policy initiatives launched by President Reagan. He also made an effort to appeal to the religious right, a loose coalition of Catholics and Protestants committed to a conservative social agenda that included opposition to abortion and gay rights and support for school prayer and censorship of pornography. But despite his best efforts, Bush

ACCEPTANCE SPEECH

. . . I respect-old fashioned common sense, and have no great love for the imaginings of social planners. I like what's been tested and found to be true. For instance:

Should public school teachers be required to lead our children in the Pledge of Allegiance? My opponent says no—but I say yes.

Should society be allowed to impose the death penalty on those who commit crimes of extraordinary cruelty and violence? My opponent says no—but I say yes.

Should free men and women have the right to own a gun to protect their home? My opponent says no—but I say yes.

Is it right to believe in the sanctity of life and protect the lives of innocent children? My opponent says no—but I say yes. We must change from abortion—to adoption. . . .

I'm the one who believes it is a scandal to give a weekend furlough to a hardened first-degree killer who hasn't even served enough time to be eligible for parole.

I'm the one who says a drug dealer who is responsible for the death of a policeman should be subject to capital punishment.

I'm the one who won't raise taxes. My opponent now says he'll raise them as a last resort, or a third resort. When a politician talks like that, you know that's one resort he'll be checking into. My opponent won't rule out raising taxes. But I will. The Congress will push me to raise taxes, and I'll say no, and they'll push, and I'll say no, and they'll push again, and I'll say to them, "Read my lips: No new taxes." . . .

• *George Bush received the nomination for president at the Republican Convention in New Orleans on 18 August 1988. His acceptance speech set the tone for the campaign. His pledge not to raise taxes haunted him because, in 1990, he implemented the second highest tax increase in U.S. history.*

trailed his Democratic opponent, Michael Dukakis of Massachusetts, in early opinion polls. To undermine his opponent's support, Bush ignored his

"In the mythology of India two young men, vying for the love of a lady, lose their heads in a bloody sword fight. The heads are hastily sewn back, but on the wrong bodies. The Legend of the Transposed Heads is also the story of the 1988 U.S. presidential election.

Approaching the Democratic convention, Michael Dukakis was likened to Zorba the Greek facing Ronald Reagan's vice president struggling with the wimp factor that so often accompanies that job.

Zorba vs. the Wimp: The Democratic dream campaign. But it was not to be. The reputation of American presidential elections for volatility, unpredictability and drama was reconfirmed. In the course of three remarkable months in the fall of 1988 the two candidates, seemingly by mutual consent, transposed images. Michael Dukakis would return to his job as governor of Massachusetts and George Bush would become the forty-first President of the United States. Zorba became the wimp; the wimp became President."

• *Robert Squier, "1988," in* Running for President, The Candidates and Their Images, *edited by Arthur M. Schlesinger, Jr.*

own call for a "kinder, gentler nation" and went on the attack, charging that Dukakis was an unpatriotic, fringe liberal who did not support the military, would raise taxes, and was weak on crime. To illustrate the last point, the Bush campaign ran ads suggesting that Dukakis was responsible for the release of Willie Horton, an African American convicted murderer who had raped a white woman while on leave from a Massachusetts prison. Bush's

GET OUT OF JAIL FREE

Michael Dukakis's furlough plan allowed convicted murderers to take a weekend leave from prison. One, Willie Horton, left and never came back. Instead he viciously raped and beat a woman while her fiancée was forced to helplessly listen to her screams.

This is only one example of many. In the last several years, Mike Dukakis has furloughed more than one murderer per day.

Mike Dukakis is the killer's best friend, and the decent, honest citizens' worst enemy.

COMPLIMENTS OF MICHAEL DUKAKIS

• *The above was printed as though it were a Monopoly card and distributed by the College Republican National Committee.* © *1988 CRNC.*

tactics proved successful. Bush won 40 states and 53.4 percent of the popular vote. In the Electoral College, he won 426 votes to 111 for Dukakis.

As president, Bush faced a difficult situation, since the Democrats continued to control both houses of Congress. During his term in office, despite numerous efforts to reach consensus, Bush had to fall back on the presidential veto to block legislation he opposed. By mid-1992, he had vetoed 28 bills, and the Democrats, despite their majority status, were unable to pull together sufficient votes to override any of them.

FOREIGN POLICY. As communism crumbled in Central and Eastern Europe (1989–1990), foreign policy became the administration's top priority, and Bush proved more decisive and successful in that area than in domestic affairs. He won significant public support for his backing of Soviet President Mikhail Gorbachev through Gorbachev's

Bush and Soviet President Mikhail Gorbachev signed the Strategic Arms Reduction Treaty (START) in July 1992. START called for major reductions in nuclear weapons. START II was signed by Bush and Russian President Boris Yeltsin (shown here) in 1993 in the Kremlin. (Courtesy Bush Presidential Materials Project.)

removal in an August 1991 coup d'état (overthrow) and his subsequent return to power. The public also approved Bush's support of sanctions against South Africa. However, he brought upon himself the criticism of human rights advocates for his more moderate stance in response to China's crackdown on student demonstrations in spring 1989.

The end of the cold war did not significantly change the administration's defense policies. Bush continued to push for increases in strategic military spending and refused to end nuclear weapons tests. Nor was he reluctant to use military force to protect U.S. interests. In December 1989, he sent

U.S. troops to invade Panama and depose its president, General Manuel Noriega. The following August, in response to Iraq's invasion of Kuwait, Bush dispatched U.S. troops to the Persian Gulf region. Condemning the Iraqi invasion of the small and nearly defenseless nation and expressing concern about Iraq's efforts to control world oil reserves, Bush convinced Congress in January 1991 to approve the use of "all necessary means" to restore order in the Persian Gulf. In February, a U.S.-led air and ground assault drove the Iraqi military forces from Kuwait. While critics noted that the Iraqi dictator Saddam Hussein remained in

Iraq invaded Kuwait early in August 1990. Later that month Bush condemned the invasion. This was a press conference about the war at Kennebunkport, Maine with Secretary of Defense Richard Cheney (left) and General Colin Powell, Head of the Joint Chiefs of Staff. (Courtesy Bush Presidential Materials Project.)

power, the Gulf War was viewed as a major U.S. victory, and Bush's popularity soared.

DOMESTIC POLICY. In domestic policy, he proved both more cautious and significantly less successful. In the face of a growing federal deficit, Bush abandoned his "Read my lips: No new taxes" campaign pledge. In January 1990, he implemented a $4 billion a year payroll tax increase and in June called for more substantial tax increases, ending up with the second largest tax increase in U.S. history. Although the tax increase was supported by both parties, it was not popular

politically. This was particularly true among conservative Republicans who had supported Bush's campaign proposal to lower the tax rate on income from capital gains. Moreover, despite the tax hike, the deficit continued to grow, reaching $200 billion in 1990 and around $300 billion in 1991. In large part this was due to the staggering costs of covering taxpayer-insured deposits at failed savings and loan institutions. Meanwhile, the economy slowed dramatically in 1989, and the nation slipped into recession in 1990. As the recession continued in 1991, Bush resisted increasing public spending to stimulate recovery but instead advocated other economic solutions. These included lowering short-term interest rates and relaxing limits on risky bank loans. When these efforts did not work and the economic slump continued, Bush's public approval ratings dropped, leaving him open to challengers from within his own party in the 1992 primaries.

Bush proved somewhat more successful in carrying out his campaign pledge to the religious right. Although he was not able to achieve many of the right's specific goals, such as a constitutional amendment to outlaw flag burning, he did manage to appoint to the Supreme Court conservative judges who could be expected to vote to overturn the Court's earlier, more liberal rulings on pornography and abortion. When a seat on the Supreme Court came open in 1990, the President nominated David H. Souter, a little-known federal judge from New Hampshire. He was easily confirmed. Then in 1991, Thurgood Marshall, the only African American on the Court, announced his retirement. Bush nominated as his successor Clarence Thomas, a conservative African American federal appeals

President Bush introduced Judge Clarence Thomas at a press conference at his home in Kennebunkport, Maine. The conservative Thomas replaced Justice Thurgood Marshall, who retired from the Supreme Court.

(Courtesy Bush Presidential Materials Project.)

THE STATE OF THE UNION, 1992

. . . We gather tonight at a dramatic and deeply promising time in our history, and in the history of man on earth.

For in the past twelve months the world has known changes of almost biblical proportions. And even now, months after the failed coup that doomed a failed system, I am not sure we have absorbed the full impact, the full import of what happened. But communism died this year.

Even as President, with the most fascinating possible vantage point, there were times when I was so busy helping to manage progress, and lead change, that I didn't always show the joy that was in my heart.

But the biggest thing that has happened in the world in my life—in our lives—is this: By the grace of God, America has won the Cold War

I mean to speak this evening of the changes that can take place in our country now that we can stop making the sacrifices we had to make when we had an avowed enemy that was a Superpower. Now we can look homeward even more, and move to set right what needs to be set right.

I will speak of those things. But let me tell you something I've been thinking these past few months. It's a kind of rollcall of honor. For the Cold War didn't "end"—it was won.

And I think of those who won it. In places like Korea, and Vietnam. And some of them didn't come back. Back then they were heroes, but this year they became what they didn't know they were: victors. . . .

• *Communist governments fell in Poland, Czechoslovakia, Hungary, and in other countries in Eastern Europe during President Bush's administration. When he left office, the only remaining communist countries were China, Cuba, and North Vietnam.*

court judge. The Thomas nomination proved anything but easy, for a former staff member, in nationally televised hearings, accused Thomas of sexual harassment. Nevertheless, Bush maintained his support for Thomas, and the U.S. Senate approved his appointment by a vote of 52 to 48.

By 1992, Bush faced opposition within his own party from conservatives unhappy with his failure to carry forward the Reagan agenda. Although he was able to defeat several challengers and win renomination, he had to make concessions to his opponents, including giving visibility in the convention to the far right and its agenda. In the general election, Bush faced not only a Democratic opponent, Bill Clinton, the governor of Arkansas, but also a third-party candidate,

Ross Perot, a Texas businessman who mounted an antigovernment campaign. Bush tried to raise questions about the "character" of his opponents and to emphasize his success in foreign policy, but he fell vulnerable to charges from both Clinton and Perot that he had mismanaged the economy. Clinton won the three-way race with 43 percent of the popular vote, compared to 37 percent for Bush and 19 percent for Perot.

George and Barbara Bush returned to Houston, Texas in January 1993. Both have written memoirs, have lectured widely, and serve on the boards of various foundations. The former President has also overseen the establishment of the Bush library at Texas A & M University in College Station, Texas.

VICE PRESIDENT

John Danforth (Dan) Quayle
(1947–)

CHRONOLOGICAL EVENTS

1947	Born, Indianapolis, Indiana, 4 February
1969	Graduated from DePauw University, Indiana
1969	Enlisted in the Indiana National Guard
1974	Graduated Indiana University, Indianapolis, Law School
1976	Elected to U.S. House of Representatives
1980	Elected to U.S. Senate
1988	Elected vice president

BIOGRAPHY

Dan Quayle divided his childhood between Indiana and Arizona, where his family owned newspapers. Graduating from DePauw University during the Vietnam War, he spent six months in the Indiana National Guard. He attended law school and married a fellow student, Marilyn Tucker. Passing their bar exams on the same day, they settled in Huntington, Indiana to practice law together.

Young, personable, and conservative, Quayle was recruited by the local Republican chairman to run for Congress. In 1976, he upset an incumbent Democrat to win a seat in the U.S. House of Representatives. In 1980, he upset another incumbent Democrat to advance to the U.S. Senate.

With Republicans in the majority, Quayle chaired a Labor Committee subcommittee. He collaborated with the liberal Democrat Edward Kennedy to enact a retraining program for industrial workers. This act was particularly beneficial to industrial areas in Indiana and helped him win reelection by a wide margin.

In the Senate, Quayle frequently met with Vice President George Bush, who planned to campaign for president in 1988. At age 64, Bush saw Quayle as a running mate who would appeal to younger voters. To build suspense for the convention, however, Bush kept his choice secret until the last minute. The press had to scramble to learn about Quayle's background. Reporters raised questions about his academic record and his avoidance of combat during the Vietnam War. Quayle's casual speaking style also made him sound unprepared. When he compared his youth and inexperience to John F. Kennedy's, his vice presidential rival Lloyd Bentsen replied, "Senator, you are no Jack Kennedy."

President Bush made a point of seeing his vice president almost daily. Quayle was invited to most major meetings, and he traveled widely to speak for the administration. He chaired the National Space Council and the Council on Competitiveness and lobbied conservative members of Congress to win votes for Bush's programs. Yet even though political reporters began to treat him more respectfully, Quayle remained the target of popular jokes. He further undermined his image by criticizing a television comedy series for promoting single parenthood and by misspelling "potato" during a school spelling bee.

When Bush and Quayle ran for reelection, they lost a three-way race to Arkansas Governor Bill Clinton. Out of office, Quayle considered running for president in 1996 but decided against it.

THE CABINET

SECRETARY OF STATE
James A. Baker, III, 1989
Lawrence S. Eagleburger, 1992

SECRETARY OF THE TREASURY
Nicholas F. Brady, 1989

ATTORNEY GENERAL
Richard Thornburgh, 1989
William Barr, 1991

SECRETARY OF THE INTERIOR
Manuel Lujan, Jr., 1989

SECRETARY OF AGRICULTURE
Clayton Yeutter, 1989
Edward R. Madigan, 1991

SECRETARY OF COMMERCE
Robert A. Mosbacher, 1989
Barbara A. Franklin, 1992

SECRETARY OF LABOR
Elizabeth H. Dole, 1989
Lynn Martin, 1991

SECRETARY OF DEFENSE
Richard B. Cheney, 1989

SECRETARY OF HOUSING AND URBAN DEVELOPMENT
Jack F. Kemp, 1989

SECRETARY OF TRANSPORTATION
Samuel K. Skinner, 1989
Andrew H. Card, 1992

SECRETARY OF ENERGY
James Watkins, 1989

SECRETARY OF HEALTH AND HUMAN SERVICES
Louis W. Sullivan, 1989

SECRETARY OF EDUCATION
Lauro F. Cavazos, 1989
Lamar Alexander, 1991

SECRETARY OF VETERANS AFFAIRS[1]
Edward J. Derwinski, 1989
Jesse Brown, 1993

1. Department of Veterans Affairs established 25 October 1989.

(Courtesy American Red Cross.)

Elizabeth H. Dole (1936–). Dole was appointed secretary of transportation by President Ronald Reagan in 1983. She was the first woman to hold that post.

As secretary of transportation, Dole instituted random drug testing for public transportation employees, imposed stricter safety aviation regulations, tightened security measures in the nation's airports, and promoted the use of air bags in automobiles.

In 1989, Dole was appointed secretary of labor by President George Bush. As labor secretary, she strengthened the enforcement of child labor laws and pushed for initiatives to help disadvantaged youth find jobs. She worked to increase health and safety regulations in the workplace.

In 1991, Dole resigned as secretary of labor to become president of the American Red Cross. In 1995, she received the Raoul Wallenberg Award for humanitarian service and was inducted into the National Women's Hall of Fame. She is married to Senator Robert Dole, former Senate majority leader and presidential candidate.

Richard B. Cheney (right) is shown here with President Bush and Secretary of State James A. Baker in the Cabinet Room on 18 May 1992. (Courtesy Bush Presidential Materials Project.)

Richard B. Cheney (1941–). Cheney was appointed secretary of defense by President George Bush in 1989. He had previously served as White House chief of staff in the administration of Gerald R. Ford.

As secretary of defense, Cheney started major troop cutbacks in order to increase funding for research in military technology.

In 1989, Cheney directed the U.S. invasion of Panama to remove dictator Manuel Noriega. Two years later, he supervised U.S. forces in the Persian Gulf. They were there to turn back Iraq's invasion of Kuwait.

James A. Baker (1930–). Baker was appointed secretary of state by President George Bush in 1989. He had previously served as secretary of the treasury in the administration of Ronald Reagan. In 1988, he managed George Bush's presidential campaign.

As secretary of state, Baker encouraged the Soviet Union and the East bloc to establish democratic governments, and he supported the reunification of Germany. During the Persian Gulf War (1991), Baker's diplomatic efforts successfully forged the Allied coalition. He resigned in August 1992 to direct Bush's reelection campaign.

FAMILY

CHRONOLOGICAL EVENTS

8 June 1925	Barbara Pierce born	11 February 1953	Son, John (Jeb), born
6 January 1945	Barbara Pierce married George Bush	22 January 1955	Son, Neil, born
		22 October 1956	Son, Marvin, born
6 July 1946	Son, George, born	18 August 1959	Daughter, Dorothy (Doro), born

Barbara Pierce was born in Rye, New York. Her father was the publisher of *Redbook* and *McCall's,* two popular magazines. In 1942, she met George Bush at a dance while he was home on leave from the United States Navy. Two years later, she dropped out of Smith College to marry him, when he was again home on leave.

As First Lady, she was very active in promoting adult literacy. In 1989, she helped organize the Barbara Bush Foundation for Family Literacy and served as its honorary chairperson. She wrote two books from the perspective of their two dogs: *C. Fred's Story (1984)* and *Millie's Book (1990).* The latter was a best-seller and all the royalties were donated to the Barbara Bush Foundation.

Barabara Bush is shown here with President Bush at Kennebunkport, Maine with their dog Millie. (Courtesy Bush Presidential Materials Project.)

◄ *Dorothy Bush graduated from Boston College. In 1992, she married Robert Koch, a former aide to House Democratic leader Richard Gephardt. In 1996, she gave birth to the Bush's 14th grandchild. She is shown here sledding with her father at Camp David.*
(Courtesy Bush Presidential Materials Project.)

President Bush went fishing off Kennebunkport in his speedboat, the Fidelity, *with two of his four sons. George (middle) graduated from Yale University and Harvard Business School. He was a pilot in the Texas National Guard. In 1989, he became one of the owners of the Texas Rangers. In 1995, he defeated Ann Richardson for the governorship of Texas.*

Jeb graduated from the University of Texas and later became chairman of the Republican Party in Dade County, Florida. He also served as Florida secretary of commerce under Governor Bob Martinez. He lost a close election to Lawton Chiles for the governorship of Florida.
(Courtesy Bush Presidential Materials Project.) ►

WALKER'S POINT

Kennebunkport, Maine

> *The Bush summer residence is located on the shoreline at Walker's Point. Kennebunkport is approximately 9 miles south of Biddeford. It is not open to the public.*

President Bush visited Walker's Point in Kennebunkport, Maine every summer of his life except in 1944 when he was a Navy pilot in World War II. (Courtesy Bush Presidential Materials Project.)

In 1901, President Bush's maternal grandfather, George Herbert Walker, purchased land known as Damon's Point, in Kennebunkport, Maine. He later renamed the property Walker's Point, and built the main house on a small, rocky strip of land on the water. In 1921, Dorothy Walker married George Bush's father, Prescott, and they lived at another house in the center of Walker's Point.

In 1978, that residence was damaged by a storm and later restored. Three years later, George Bush purchased the main house from George Herbert Walker's daughter-in-law. During Bush's presidency, Walker's Point was the site of numerous press conferences and meetings among world leaders. The house is closed to the public, and closely guarded by the Secret Service.

The George Bush Presidential Library Center

Texas A&M University • College Station, Texas 77843-1145 • Tel: (409) 862-2251

"In this presidential library, at Texas A&M University, you will find documentation for some of the most revolutionary changes that the world has ever seen take place. Whether it is the peace talks . . . or whether it is the unification in Germany . . . whether it is the decline and fall of the Soviet Empire . . . whether it is the historic precedence-setting coalition for Desert Storm. All of that will be reflected with accurate detail in the library for scholars to make their own conclusions." — George Bush. (Courtesy Bush Presidential Materials Project.)

The George Bush Presidential Library Center will be located in College Station on 90 acres of the Texas A&M University campus. It will contain a museum, archives, meeting rooms, classrooms, auditoriums, administrative offices, and a place for university programs. It will also provide offices and living quarters for President and Mrs. Bush.

There will be associated academic programs. The George Bush School of Government and Public Service will offer a master of public administration degree. The Center for Presidential Studies will conduct research solely on the presidency and will distribute this information to scholars, government officials and the general public. The Center for Public Leadership Studies will conduct research on understanding leadership and its development.

The design and construction of the center will be funded by private sources, as specified in federal statutes. An estimated $82 million is required for construction; of this amount, $42 million will be used for the specified library and museum. Plans called for it to open in 1997.

Bill Clinton

42ND PRESIDENT

OF THE UNITED STATES OF AMERICA

CHRONOLOGICAL EVENTS

19 August 1946	Born, Hope, Arkansas
1968	Graduated from Georgetown University, Washington, D.C.
1968–1970	Attended University of Oxford, England as Rhodes scholar
1973	Graduated from Yale University Law School, Connecticut
	Returned to Arkansas; opened law practice and taught at University of Arkansas School of Law
1974	Ran unsuccessfully for U.S. House of Representatives
1976	Elected attorney general of Arkansas
1978	Elected governor of Arkansas
1980	Ran unsuccessfully for reelection as governor of Arkansas
1982	Again elected governor of Arkansas; served 5 terms
1988	Delivered nominating speech for Michael Dukakis at Democratic National Convention
1990	Appointed chair of Democratic Leadership Council
3 November 1992	Elected president
20 January 1993	Inaugurated president
5 February 1993	Signed Family and Medical Leave Act
20 May 1993	Signed "motor voter" bill
5–6 August 1993	Secured passage of deficit reduction plan (Omnibus Budget Reconciliation Act)
22 September 1993	Unveiled universal health care reform proposal, was not passed by Congress
30 November 1993	Signed Brady bill (Brady Handgun Violence Prevention Act)
8 December 1993	Signed North American Free Trade Agreement
13 September 1994	Signed anticrime bill
8 December 1994	Signed General Agreement on Tariffs and Trade
14 December 1995	Bosnian peace agreement signed (Dayton Agreements)
22 August 1996	Signed Welfare Reform Act
5 November 1996	Reelected president
20 January 1997	Inaugurated president

BIOGRAPHY

In his campaign for election as the nation's forty-second president, William Jefferson Clinton presented himself as the candidate of hope and change. While such language is hardly unusual in political campaigns, those words had more concrete meaning in Clinton's case. He was, quite literally, the candidate of hope—he was born in Hope, Arkansas. More important, his election marked a significant change in leadership. As the first president born after World War II, he represented a generational shift, bringing to presidential politics both the advantages and the disadvantages of being part of the baby boomer generation. Baby boomers are the generation of Americans born just after World War II when the birthrate in the United States boomed or rose dramatically.

EARLY YEARS. Clinton was born on 19 August 1946, just two months after his father died in a traffic accident. Named William Jefferson Blythe IV after his father, he lived with his grandparents in Hope for two years while his widowed mother, Virginia Blythe, completed studies in New Orleans to become a nurse-anesthetist. When he was four years old, his mother married Roger Clinton, a Hot Springs, Arkansas car dealer from whom the future president took his last name. The young Clinton was a popular student leader with a strong academic record. He considered becoming a musician, a teacher, or a minister but decided on a career in politics. The deciding moment for Clinton came when he met his political idol, President John F. Kennedy, in Washington in July 1963, while attending the national convention of Boys' Nation, a leadership organization for high school students sponsored by the American Legion.

Clinton returned to Washington the next year to enter Georgetown University, from which he graduated in 1968 with a bachelor of arts degree in international studies. During his sophomore year, summer volunteer work in an Arkansas governor's campaign paid off in a job in the office of J. William Fulbright, the state's senior senator. After graduation, rather than continuing to work on Capitol Hill, Clinton accepted a Rhodes scholarship, and he attended Oxford University in England for the next two years. He declined a third year at Oxford, however, and returned to the United States to enroll in the Yale Law School, from which he graduated in 1973. Although he briefly returned to Washington to work for the House Judiciary Committee, Clinton came to the conclusion that his future lay in Arkansas. He returned

there later in 1973 to establish a private law practice and to teach at the University of Arkansas School of Law. In 1975, he married Hillary Rodham, an attorney and a former classmate at Yale. Their only child, a daughter named Chelsea Victoria, was born in 1980.

EARLY POLITICAL CAREER. In 1974, a little over a year after graduating from law school, Clinton launched his political career with a bid for a seat in the U.S. House of Representatives. Although he lost the election, he came within 4 percentage points of defeating the Republican incumbent. This marked him as a rising star within the Democratic Party. Two years later, he directed Jimmy Carter's presidential campaign in Arkansas and won election as the state's attorney general. Building on the reputation he established in that office as a consumer advocate, he ran for governor of Arkansas in 1978. He won the Democratic nomination with 59 percent of the vote in a five-person primary. His election that fall made him, at age 32, the nation's youngest governor. His triumph proved brief, however, for the voters turned him out of office in 1980, apparently unhappy over his support of increases in the gasoline tax and in automobile licensing fees to finance a highway improvement program. Voters also did not like his links to President Carter. Carter's decision to relocate Cuban refugees to the state was enormously unpopular. Clinton lost the general election in the 1980 Republican landslide that carried Arkansas for Ronald Reagan.

Clinton returned to his law practice and regrouped in preparation for a bid to regain the governor's office in 1982. Although critics dubbed him "Slick Willie" because of his efforts to undercut his opponents, he won the Democratic nomination. He then won the general election, taking the office that he would continue to hold for nearly a decade. As governor, he won national attention for his efforts to improve education in a state where the per-student expenditure was the second lowest in the nation and the average teacher's salary was the third lowest. Under

Clinton's leadership, the state raised taxes and imposed teacher competency tests in 1983, but critics maintained that these steps led to slight improvements only in education and in teacher salaries. Other initiatives included a jobs program, an infant and child health program, new highway projects, and the use of boot camps instead of prison for nonviolent first offenders. Although his critics within the state were numerous, other governors, according to a 1991 poll, viewed Clinton as one of the nation's most effective state chief executives.

During this same period, Clinton established his credentials at the national level, chairing the Education Commission of the States, the Southern Growth Policies Board, the Democratic Governors' Association, and the National Governors' Association. He even considered running for the presidency in 1988. Instead he threw his support behind fellow governor Michael Dukakis of Massachusetts. Although he had established a reputation for effectively combining old-style public speaking with solid discussion of policy, his speech for Dukakis at the Democratic National Convention in 1988 was boring and long-winded. This dimmed his rising star within the party. Over the next three years, Clinton worked hard to reestablish his reputation and to develop a stronger base of support among party moderates. Despite his liberal credentials from having managed George McGovern's presidential campaign in Texas in 1972, he joined the Democratic Leadership Council (DLC). The DLC was a group of moderates committed to countering the influence of the left and to reducing the party's identification with organized labor, racial minorities, and opponents of the military. Taking welfare reform as his central issue, Clinton served as chair of the DLC from 1990 to 1991.

President Clinton chose Vice President Albert Gore Jr. to lead the U.S. delegation to Nelson Mandela's inauguration as president of South Africa on 10 May 1994. Most of the delegation were African Americans, including Secretary of Commerce Ron Brown, Secretary of Agriculture Mike Espy, Representative Kweisi Mfume (chairman of the Congressional Black Caucus), former Federal Judge Leon Higginbotham, former New York City Mayor David Dinkins, Mrs. Coretta Scott King, Maya Angelou, Quincy Jones, and Reverend Jesse Jackson.

(Courtesy The White House; photographer: Callie Shell.)

ELECTION OF 1992. In October 1991, Clinton entered the race for the Democratic presidential nomination. He raised more funds than his opponents, put together an impressive campaign organization, and quickly moved from little-known candidate to front-runner. He claimed that his record as a moderate made him the most electable Democratic candidate. However, he proved open to

Bill Clinton appeared on more popular radio and television shows than his opponents. He put on his sunglasses and played "Heartbreak Hotel" with Posse on The Arsenio Hall Show, a late-night television show with many younger viewers. The brief segment was repeated many times on television and the saxophone became a symbol of the Clinton campaign. (Courtesy Collection of David J. and Janice L. Frent.)

attack on a number of questions about his personal life: a claim of an extramarital affair, reports that he had smoked marijuana as a student, and charges that he was a draft dodger. The last two were generational issues, raising questions about the fitness of the post–World War II generation to govern. Living up to his "Slick Willie" reputation, Clinton managed to undercut or deflect these character issues and come in a strong second in the New Hampshire primary in early 1992. His opponents fell by the wayside one by one during the primary season, ensuring Clinton's nomination before the party's convention in July. He chose as his running mate Albert Gore Jr., a senator from Tennessee and

a fellow moderate Southerner, DLC member, and baby boomer.

In his campaign against the incumbent, George Bush, Clinton claimed to represent a new generation ready to take over and restore hope to the American people.

Countering the Republicans' claim that the contest was over "family values," Clinton responded, "Our families have values. Our government doesn't." He insisted that the real issue for voters was the economy—that Bush had raised taxes on the middle class while lowering them for the wealthy and had failed to provide the leadership necessary to end the economic downturn that had plagued the nation since 1990. A sign in the Clinton campaign headquarters drove this point home: "It's the economy, stupid!" In emphasizing economic issues, Clinton's strategists assumed the continued loyalty of the party's

liberal, urban base and the need to win over moderate suburban voters. Thus Clinton supported reduction of the federal deficit and a smaller bureaucracy, welfare and health care reform, and a modest tax cut for the middle class. He also favored the shifting of funds from defense to civilian programs and investing in the nation's infrastructure (basic facilities and installations such as roads).

Bush tried to counter by labeling his opponent a "tax-and-spend liberal." He questioned whether

DEDICATION OF THE
UNITED STATES HOLOCAUST MEMORIAL MUSEUM

. . . It is my purpose on behalf of the United States to commemorate this magnificent museum, meeting as we do among memorials within the site of the memorial to Thomas Jefferson, the author of our freedom. Near where Abraham Lincoln is seated, who gave his life so that our nation might extend its mandate of freedom to all who live within our borders. We gather near the place where the legendary and recently departed Marian Anderson sang songs of freedom, and where Martin Luther King summoned us all to dream and work together. . . .

The Holocaust began when the most civilized country of its day unleashed unprecedented acts of cruelty and hatred abetted by perversions of science, philosophy, and law. . . . The merciless hordes who, themselves, were educated as others who were educated stood by and did nothing. Millions died for who they were, how they worshipped, what they believed, and who they loved. But one people—the Jews—were immutably marked for total destruction. They who were among their nation's most patriotic citizens, whose extinction served no military purpose nor offered any political gain, they who threatened no one were slaughtered by an efficient, unrelenting bureaucracy, dedicated solely to a radical evil with a curiously antiseptic title: The Final Solution.

The Holocaust reminds us forever that knowledge divorced from values can only serve to deepen the human nightmare; that a head without a heart is not humanity. . . .

Now, with the demise of communism and the rise of democracy out of the ashes of former communist states, with the end of the Cold War we must not only rejoice in so much that is good in the world, but recognize that not all in this new world is good. We learn again and again that the world has yet to run its course of animosity and violence.

Ethnic cleansing in the former Yugoslavia is but the most brutal and blatant and ever-present manifestation of what we see also with the oppression of the Kurds in Iraq, the abusive treatment of the Baha'i in Iran, the endless race-based violence in South Africa. And in many other places we are reminded again and again how fragile are the safeguards of civilization. . . .

The evil represented in this museum is incontestable. But as we are its witness, so must we remain its adversary in the world in which we live. So we must stop the fabricators of history and the bullies as well. Left unchallenged, they would still prey upon the powerless; and we must not permit that to happen again.

To build bulwarks against this kind of evil, we know there is but one path to take. It is the direction opposite that which produced the Holocaust, it is that which recognizes that among all our differences, we still cannot ever separate ourselves one from another. We must find in our diversity our common humanity. We must reaffirm that common humanity, even in the darkest and deepest of our own disagreements. . . .

On this day of triumphant reunion and celebration, I hope those who have survived have found their peace. Our task, with God's blessing upon our souls and the memories of the fallen in our hearts and minds, is to the ceaseless struggle to preserve human rights and dignity. We are now strengthened and will be forever strengthen by remembrance. I pray that we shall prevail.

President Bill Clinton made the above remarks at the dedication ceremony of the United States Holocaust Memorial Museum on 22 April 1993. The Museum is located 1,500 feet from the Washington Monument in Washington, D.C.

Henry Ross Perot was born in Texarkana, Texas in 1930. He graduated from the United States Naval Academy and served in the U.S. Navy. In 1984, Perot sold his company, Electronic Data Services, to General Motors for $2.5 billion.

Perot's running mate in 1992 was James Stockdale, a retired admiral and former prisoner of war in Vietnam. In spite of Stockdale's poor performance in the vice presidential debates, Perot received almost 20 million votes. (Courtesy Perot Reform Committee.)

the Arkansan could be trusted, given the contradictory accounts of his Vietnam War draft status and the questions about his record as governor of Arkansas. Both men in turn tried to turn aside the challenge from the third-party candidate H. Ross Perot, a Texas billionaire businessman. Perot's folksy wit and insistence on the necessity of deficit reduction appealed to many voters. Although Perot won 19 percent of the vote—the largest for any third-party candidate since 1912—the election results otherwise proved consistent with campaign polls, with Clinton winning 43 percent of the popular vote to Bush's 37 percent. In the Electoral College, Clinton won 370 electoral votes to Bush's 168.

DOMESTIC POLICY. Although Clinton enjoyed a 60 percent approval rating when he took office in January 1993, much of that good will was quickly wasted as he and his aides became bogged down in a series of divisive issues and problematic appointments. He quickly fulfilled his promise to end the Reagan-era prohibition on discussion of abortion in federally funded clinics. However, he met stiff resistance when he tried to end the barring of homosexuals from military service. He ended up compromising his position and alienating people on both sides of the issue. Cabinet and other high-level appointments also proved surprisingly difficult and time-consuming for the new President, particularly when it came to women and minorities. The Clinton administration appeared surprisingly inept, announcing the appointment of individuals whose names later had to be withdrawn as various personal and political problems were uncovered.

Clinton proved no more skillful in his efforts to address the nation's economic problems. Although a key element of his campaign platform had been a middle-class tax cut, he proposed instead to stimulate the economy through programs that would have most benefited low-income urban minorities. Congress rejected those programs but narrowly passed his deficit reduction plan. This plan called for saving $496 billion over five years and gave priority to fiscal responsibility over economic recovery. During the campaign he had also called for health care reform, and that became a high-profile issue when he appointed his wife to head a task force charged with developing a plan. In October 1993, Hillary Clinton's task force submitted a proposal for universal coverage under a managed-care system. Congress killed the plan in the face of opposition from within the health care industry and concerns about the costs of the plan to individuals and small businesses. Clinton made even less progress in fulfilling his promise of campaign finance reform.

He was more successful with proposals to make it easier for people to register to vote, to provide

President Clinton signed the so-called "motor voter" bill on 20 May 1993. The bill requires states to allow those applying for driver's licenses to register to vote. At the signing ceremony, President Clinton said, "Now there is no longer the excuse of the difficulty of registration." (Courtesy Library of Congress.)

leave for workers with new children or sick family members, to raise the minimum wage, to link federal financial aid for college students to national service, and to crack down on crime. The last included the passage of a bill (the Brady bill) in 1993 that required a waiting period and a background check for handgun buyers. He also signed a broader, bipartisan anticrime bill in 1994 that banned many types of assault weapons and provided federal funds for prison construction, the hiring of additional police officers, and crime prevention programs. Although he had called for the restructuring of the welfare system in his 1992 campaign, Clinton vetoed two reform bills passed in 1995 and 1996 by the Republican-controlled Congress but then signed a third in August 1996. That bill constituted the most radical overhaul of the welfare system in 60 years, and Clinton's signing of it angered many liberal Democrats who feared its impact on the nation's poor.

FOREIGN POLICY. In foreign policy matters, Clinton initially seemed uncertain and ill informed. He had criticized Bush during the campaign for denying asylum to Haitian political refugees but then as president continued his predecessor's policy. Despite the opposition of some members of his own party, he also successfully pushed for passage of the North American Free Trade Agreement. This agreement phased out tariffs on trade among the United States, Mexico, and Canada. He proved more decisive and gathered more support for his efforts to stop the Iraqi military buildup in October 1994 and to halt North Korea's development of nuclear weapons, for negotiating freer world trade under the General Agreement on Tariffs and Trade, for the administration's peace efforts in the Middle East, and for his opposition to the military dictatorship in Haiti. The dominant foreign policy issue in 1995 proved to be the civil war in Bosnia. Clinton won approval

Prime Minister Yitzhak Rabin (left) and PLO Chairman Yasir Arafat shook hands at the White House in September 1993. There they sealed the agreement to hold peace talks between Israel and Palestine.

By 1996, Rabin had been assassinated and violence and bloodshed had broken out in the Gaza Strip and the West Bank. On 1 October 1996, Arafat met with the recently elected prime minister of Israel, Benjamin Netanyahu, in Washington. King Saddam Hussein of Iraq also took part in the talks which had been arranged by President Bill Clinton. (Courtesy The White House.)

President Bill Clinton and British Prime Minister John Major met at the White House on 24 February 1993. Prime Minister Major said that he welcomed the President's initiative to deliver humanitarian help to Bosnia. (Courtesy The White House.)

for his role in engineering a peace agreement among the warring parties, but there was considerable opposition to his commitment of U.S. troops to implement the accord (known as the Dayton Agreements).

THE CHARACTER ISSUE. Throughout his administration, Clinton battled questions about his integrity. He faced a sexual harassment suit by an Arkansas woman, claims regarding his wife's commodity trading activities and her role in firing White House travel office personnel, and investigations by Congress and by a special prosecutor into his and his wife's participation in the Whitewater Development Corporation, a failed real estate venture. The related suicide of Vince Foster, a top aide, and the clouded resignations of three senior members of his administration further complicated the

situation. These issues not only proved damaging to the public's opinion of the President but also kept the Clinton administration from pursuing a more substantial agenda.

1994 MID-TERM ELECTIONS. By fall 1994, Clinton's approval ratings had declined significantly, and the Republicans found him a useful campaign target in congressional elections. They labeled him as a tax-and-spend liberal who lacked decisiveness and credibility. They said that he had failed to address the concerns of the middle class. The tactic worked, and the Republican Party not only gained control of Congress for the first time in four decades but also won a majority of the nation's governorships (including the governorships of seven of the eight most populous states) for the first time since the Depression of the 1930s.

President Clinton's efforts to work with the new Republican majority failed. He is shown here with Senate Majority Leader Robert Dole (left) and Speaker of the House Newt Gingrich. (Courtesy Library of Congress.)

Claiming a popular mandate to undo decades of Democratic social legislation and big government, the new Republican Congress focused initially on the conservative agenda put forth in the "Contract with America," a ten-part campaign pledge made by House Republican candidates. The Contract called for changes in welfare, defense, Social Security, tax regulations, and crime prevention programs; legislation to reduce the power of the federal government, including a prohibition on congressionally imposed mandates on the states without adequate funding; and amendments to the Constitution to require a balanced federal budget and to establish term limits for members of Congress. While House Republicans fulfilled their pledge to take action on every point in the Contract within the first hundred days of the new Congress, their flurry of action yielded only six laws and did not bring about the promised dramatic reduction in federal power or cuts in federal spending.

Clinton at first tried to work with the new Republican majority but soon shifted ground, vetoing 11 bills over the course of 1995, the first vetoes of his presidency (only one of which was overridden). In the fall, differences between Democrats and Republicans intensified as the latter aggressively pursued a seven-year deficit reduction plan that balanced a sizable middle-class tax cut with reductions in health care entitlements, welfare, and other domestic programs. When Congress failed to deliver any of the 13 annual appropriations bills to Clinton prior to the beginning of the new fiscal year on 1 October 1995, the White House and Congress reached a stalemate over terms for keeping the government operating. While Congress insisted that the President commit to balancing the budget in seven years, Clinton refused to agree to the Republicans' funding priorities. When negotiations broke down, the federal government shut down twice. The second shutdown was of record duration and extended into 1996. Clinton held his ground, and the budget standoff ended only when congressional Republicans dropped their seven-year budget plan in late winter.

ELECTION OF 1996. As he began the last year of his term, Clinton appeared to be the chief beneficiary of the Republicans' "revolution"—his standing in public opinion polls far exceeded that

President Bill Clinton is pictured here with Kweisi Mfume, president of the National Association for the Advancement of Colored People (NAACP). The NAACP is the oldest civil rights organization in the United States.

President Clinton and Senator Robert Dole were both invited to speak at the 1996 NAACP convention. Clinton accepted but Dole turned down the invitation. He first blamed a scheduling conflict. He later admitted that he was afraid that he was being "set up" by Mr. Mfume. Mfume was a five-term Democratic Congressman from Baltimore, Maryland and the former chairman of the Congressional Black Caucus. (Courtesy The White House.)

ACCEPTANCE SPEECH AT DEMOCRATIC NATIONAL CONVENTION

. . . Now, here's the main idea: I love and revere the rich and proud history of America. And I am determined to take our best traditions into the future. But with all respect, we do not need to build a bridge to the past. We need to build a bridge to the future. And that is what I commit to you to do.

So tonight—tonight let us resolve to build that bridge to the 21st century, to meet our challenges and protect our values. Let us build a bridge to help our parents raise their children, to help young people and adults to get the education and training they need, to make our streets safer, to help Americans succeed at home and at work, to break the cycle of poverty and dependence, to protect our environment for generations to come, and to maintain our world leadership for peace and freedom. Let us resolve to build that bridge. . . .

I want to build a bridge to the 21st century in which we expand opportunity through education, where computers are as much a part of the classroom as blackboards, where highly-trained teachers demand peak performance from our students, where every eight-year-old can point to a book and say, I can read it myself. . . .

My fellow Americans, let me say one last time, we can only build our bridge to the 21st century if we build it together, and if we're willing to walk arm and arm across that bridge together. . . .

We have seen the terrible, terrible price that people pay when they insist on fighting and killing their neighbors over their differences. In our own country we have seen America pay a terrible price for any form of discrimination. And we have seen us grow stronger as we have steadily let more and more of our hatreds and our fears go; as we have given more and more of our people the chance to live their dreams. . . .

So look around here, look around here—old or young, healthy as a horse or a person with a disability that hasn't kept you down, man or woman, Native American, native born, immigrant, straight or gay—whatever; the test ought to be I believe in the Constitution, the Bill of Rights and the Declaration of Independence. I believe in religious liberty. I believe in freedom of speech. I believe in working hard and playing by the rules. I'm showing up for work tomorrow. I'm building that bridge to the 21st century. That ought to be the test.

My fellow Americans, 68 nights from tonight the American people will face once again a critical moment of decision. . . . The real choice is whether we will build a bridge to the future or a bridge to the past; about whether we believe our best days are still out there or our best days are behind us; about whether we want a country of people all working together or one where you're on your own.

Let us commit ourselves this night to rise up and build the bridge we know we ought to build all the way to the 21st century. Let us have faith—and let us have faith—faith—American faith that we are not leaving our greatness behind. We're going to carry it right on with us into that new century—a century of new challenge and unlimited promise.

Let us, in short, do the work that is before us, so that when our time here is over, we will all watch the sun go down—as we all must—and say truly, we have prepared our children for the dawn. . . .

President Bill Clinton delivered this speech at the Democratic National Convention in Chicago, Illinois on 29 August 1996. Senator Robert Dole had made the point in his acceptance speech that he was a bridge to the past. President Clinton countered by saying that what was needed was a bridge to the future.

DOLE★KEMP

Paid For By Dole/Kemp '96

Robert Dole (right) was severely wounded in Italy during World War II. He went to the University of Arizona through the GI bill and received a law degree from Washburn Municipal College in Kansas. Dole was elected to the U.S. House of Representatives in 1960 and to the U.S. Senate in 1968. President Gerald R. Ford chose him as his vice presidential running mate in 1976. In 1994, Dole was elected U.S. Senate majority leader for the 104th Congress. He received the presidential nomination at the Republican Convention in San Diego, California on 15 August 1996. He resigned from the Senate on 11 June 1996. (Courtesy Dole/Kemp '96.) ▶

◀ *Senator Robert Dole chose Jack Kemp (left) as his running mate. In 1960, Kemp was signed to play quarterback for the Los Angeles (later San Diego) Chargers in the old American Football League. He was traded to the Buffalo Bills. He served in the U.S. House of Representatives from 1970 through 1988. Kemp sought the Republican nomination in 1987 but withdrew. President George Bush named him Secretary of Housing and Urban Development (HUD) in 1989. Kemp endorsed Steve Forbes, Dole's main opponent, in the 1996 primaries.* (Courtesy Dole/Kemp '96.)

(Courtesy Clinton/Gore '96.)

When I ran for President four years ago, no challenge loomed larger or seemed more difficult to solve than the deficit. The deficit had soared to $290 billion, a record high and growing.

In the 12 years before I took office, our national debt had quadrupled over what it had accumulated for the 200 years before.

We worked hard to change that. We passed a tough economic plan without a single solitary vote on the other side. My opponent and others said we could never reduce the deficit. They said we would wreck the economy. They said these tough decisions would bring no good. . . . we know now that for four years in a row, we have reduced the deficit. That's the first time a President has reduced the deficit in all four years of a term in the twentieth century. . . .

The deficit was a ball and chain holding back our economy. Well, today we got some new good news about exactly how far the deficit has dropped since I took office. . . . The 1996 deficit has been cut to $107 billion. That's a reduction of 63 percent. That's the lowest level since 1981. But when you adjust for inflation, it is the lowest deficit in 22 years. . . .

Today the United States has a deficit in its budget that, as a percentage of our income, is lower than that of any other major industrial nation on the face of the Earth.

In a series of speeches during the closing days of the 1996 presidential race, President Clinton focused on the economy and pointed to figures that showed that the federal deficit had dropped to its lowest levels since 1981, the first year of the Ronald Reagan administration. He made these comments in University City, Missouri on 28 October 1996.

of Congress or of his rivals for the presidency within their party. For Clinton, the future depended on the extent to which he could position himself as a centrist capable of leading the nation and portray his Republican opponents as obstructionists incapable of governing. Toward that end, he recruited the same political consultant who had orchestrated his 1982 political resurrection. More focused and better positioned to deflect Republican critics, Clinton quickly secured a sizable lead in the polls over his Republican opponent, Robert Dole, former U.S. senator from Kansas.

Clinton called for "a bridge to the 21st century" rather than his opponent's call for a bridge to the past. Clinton campaigned once again as the representative of a new generation in U.S. politics. The Dole campaign never really seemed to get off the ground, while Clinton enjoyed the advantages of incumbency and a prosperous economy.

The election results confirmed Clinton's political comeback. He won with 49 percent of the popular vote, compared to 41 percent for Dole and 8 percent for Perot. Perot's popular vote was less than half his 1992 vote. In the Electoral College, Clinton won 379 votes to Dole's 159. Clinton became the first Democrat since Franklin D. Roosevelt to win a second term as president. At age 50, he also became the youngest president ever to win reelection.

On the day after the election, President Clinton started to build a new team. Many of the members of the cabinet were expected to resign to pursue other activities. White House Chief of Staff, Leon Panetta, was expected to return to his home in California, perhaps to run for governor.

The Republicans held control of both houses of Congress. The Senate Minority Leader Tom Daschle (Democrat, South Dakota) said of the message sent by the voters, "If there is a mandate, it is to govern from the middle and take things slowly. They want us to work together and solve our nation's problems and cut the partisanship."

(From left to right) Bill and Hillary Clinton and Albert and Tipper Gore. The Clinton-Gore ticket won the 1996 election with 49% of the popular vote and 379 electoral votes compared to 159 for Dole and Kemp. (Courtesy Library of Congress.)

VICE PRESIDENT

Albert Arnold Gore Jr.
(1948–)

CHRONOLOGICAL EVENTS

1948	Born, Washington, D.C., 31 March
1969	Graduated from Harvard University,
1969	Enlisted in the U.S. Army
1976	Elected to U.S. House of Representatives
1984	Elected to U.S. Senate
1992	Elected vice president
1996	Reelected vice president, 5 November
1997	Inaugurated vice president, 20 January

BIOGRAPHY

Born and raised in Washington, D.C., Albert Gore Jr. seemed groomed for a career in politics. His father, Albert Gore Sr., served as a liberal Democratic representative and senator from Tennessee. The younger Gore attended St. Alban's School and Harvard University. In 1969, his father's Republican opponent pointed to the younger Gore as an Ivy Leaguer who had escaped the draft. Although he opposed the Vietnam War, Gore felt obligated to enlist. He served in Vietnam as an army journalist.

He returned to become an investigative reporter for the *Nashville Tennessean*. Helped by his family name, Gore was elected to the U.S. House of Representatives in 1976. After four terms in the House, he won a seat in the U.S. Senate in 1984. An earnest and diligent legislator, he specialized in environmental protection, population control, women's rights, and the "information superhighway."

In 1988, Gore campaigned for the Democratic nomination for president as a moderately liberal Southerner. His wooden style generated little enthusiasm, and he withdrew from the race. The next year, his six-year-old son, Albert III, was hit by a car and seriously injured. The incident caused Gore to reevaluate his ambitions. In 1992, he decided against running again for president in order to spend more time with his family.

Arkansas Governor Bill Clinton received the Democratic nomination that year and chose Gore for his vice presidential running mate. The two did not balance the ticket in the traditional sense since they were the same age, came from the same region, and shared similar political outlooks. They presented themselves as a "New Generation" ticket that promised youth, energy, change, and vision. Campaigning together by bus, Clinton and Gore built a friendly relationship that carried into their administration.

As vice president, Gore exerted influence on a broad range of issues and appointments. In domestic policy, he brought together major automakers to discuss ways of producing environmentally safe cars. He also headed an effort to "reinvent" government by making the federal bureaucracy smaller and more efficient. He conducted special foreign missions, most notably persuading Ukraine to destroy its stockpile of nuclear weapons. Gore cleverly sidestepped such controversial issues as the administration's losing fight for health care reform. Respecting Gore's judgment, President Clinton rarely made a major decision without consulting him.

THE CABINET

SECRETARY OF STATE
Warren M. Christopher, 1993

SECRETARY OF THE TREASURY
Lloyd M. Bentsen, 1993
Robert E. Rubin, 1995

ATTORNEY GENERAL
Janet Reno, 1993

SECRETARY OF THE INTERIOR
Bruce Babbitt, 1993

SECRETARY OF AGRICULTURE
Mike Espy, 1993
Dan Glickman, 1995

SECRETARY OF COMMERCE
Ronald H. Brown, 1993
Mickey Kantor, 1996

SECRETARY OF LABOR
Robert B. Reich, 1993

SECRETARY OF DEFENSE
Les Aspin, 1993
William J. Perry, 1994

SECRETARY OF HOUSING AND URBAN DEVELOPMENT
Henry G. Cisneros, 1993

SECRETARY OF TRANSPORTATION
Federico F. Peña

SECRETARY OF ENERGY
Hazel R. O'Leary, 1993

SECRETARY OF HEALTH AND HUMAN SERVICES
Donna E. Shalala, 1993

SECRETARY OF EDUCATION
Richard W. Riley, 1993

SECRETARY OF VETERANS AFFAIRS
Jesse Brown, 1993

Janet Reno is shown here with President Bill Clinton.
(Courtesy Library of Congress.)

Janet Reno (1938–). Reno was appointed attorney general by President Bill Clinton in 1993. At the time of her appointment, she was serving as attorney general for Florida. She was the first woman to hold the post of attorney general.

Attorney General Reno and the Bureau of Alcohol, Tobacco, and Firearms (ATF) were widely criticized for the biggest raid in its history on 28 February 1993. Sixteen ATF agents were wounded and four ATF agents and six religious zealots, known as Branch Davidians, were killed in Waco, Texas. Two months later, the FBI moved in with tanks and tear gas. The fire that resulted killed the Davidian's leader, David Koresh, and most of his followers, including 25 children.

Many people who testified at the congressional hearings on this tragedy felt that it could have been avoided if federal law enforcement agencies had not made so many mistakes.

Reno supported the passage of the Freedom of Access to Clinic Entrances Act (1994), which made it a federal crime to block the entrances of abortion clinics, to destroy clinic property, to injure employees, or to assault patients. She also supported the controversial Crime Law (1994), which provided for the hiring of 100,000 new police officers, the building of more prisons, and community programs to prevent crime.

(Courtesy U.S. Department of Commerce.)

Ronald H. Brown (1941–1996). Ron Brown spent his childhood among the black and white elite of New York City. His father managed the famous Hotel Theresa in the heart of Harlem. He graduated from Middlebury College, Vermont and served for four years in the U.S. Army in Germany and Korea. He earned a law degree at night from St. John's University, New York while working as a welfare caseworker.

Brown was involved in the civil rights movement in the late 1960s and for a dozen years he championed civil rights with the National Urban League. He was chief counsel to the Senate Judiciary Committee under the chairmanship of Senator Edward M. Kennedy. In 1992, he served as chairman of the Democratic National Committee.

Under Secretary Brown's leadership, the Commerce Department became the powerhouse envisioned by President Bill Clinton. Secretary Brown promoted U.S. exports and technologies. He led trade development missions to five continents. During his tenure, U.S. exports reached a record high.

Secretary Brown was killed in an airplane crash in April 1996 while on a trade mission to Bosnia. He was leading a group of business executives seeking a role in the postwar reconstuction of the former Yugoslavia. President Clinton called him a "magnificent life-force" who "walked and ran and flew throughout life."

(Courtesy U.S. Department of State.)

Warren M. Christopher (1925–). Christopher was appointed secretary of state by President Bill Clinton in 1993. At the time of his appointment, he was chairman of the law firm, O'Melveny & Myers.

Christopher served as deputy attorney general during the administration of Lyndon B. Johnson and deputy secretary of state during the administration of Jimmy Carter. As deputy secretary, he helped negotiate the release of 52 American hostages in Iran. He also headed the first interagency group on human rights. In 1981, he was awarded the Medal of Freedom, the nation's highest civilian award.

In 1991, Christopher served as chairman of the commission that investigated the Los Angeles Police Department in the aftermath of the Rodney King incident. The following year he served as the director of the presidential transition team for Bill Clinton.

As secretary of state, he met with the leaders of Israel and Lebanon to help limit fighting and stop attacks on civilians in the Middle East. He also negotiated an anti-terrorism pact with Israel. In 1996, he was a dynamic force behind the success of the Dayton Agreements, the peace talks between the warring parties in Bosnia-Herzegovina. He also was involved in the extension of the North American Aerospace Defense Command (NORAD). This agreement called for joint work between the United States and Canada on new technologies in aerospace defenses.

In fall 1996, Christopher worked tirelessly with Prime Minister Benjamin Netanyahu of Israel and Palestinian Chairman Yasir Arafat to keep the peace talks going after violence broke out in the Gaza Strip and the West Bank.

Christopher was one of President Clinton's closest advisors. On election day in 1996, Christopher told the President that he intended to resign soon after Inauguration Day.

Donna E. Shalala (1941-). Shalala was appointed secretary of health and human services by President Bill Clinton in 1993. She had previously served as assistant secretary for policy development and research at the Department of Housing and Urban Development during the administration of Jimmy Carter. At the time of her appointment, she was chancellor of the University of Wisconsin. She was the first woman to head a Big Ten university.

Shalala, a leading scholar on the political economy of state and local governments, was named one of the most experienced and successful public managers in the country by Business Week in 1992.

As secretary of health and human services, Shalala concentrated on reforming the nation's welfare system and improving health care while containing health costs. She supported increased funding for biomedical research and a tightening up on scientific waste and fraud. She also supported President Clinton's decision to sign the Welfare Reform Act of 1996, and she promised to work with President Clinton for changes in the law. Under her leadership the Department of Health and Human services was reorganized and the office of the assistant secretary for health was eliminated.

(Courtesy U.S. Department of Health and Human Services.)

FAMILY

CHRONOLOGICAL EVENTS

26 October 1947	Hillary Rodham born
11 October 1975	Hillary Rodham married Bill Clinton
27 February 1980	Daughter, Chelsea Victoria, born

(Courtesy The White House.)

Hillary Rodham was born in Chicago, Illinois. She was the eldest child and only daughter of Hugh E. Rodham, an owner of a textile company, and Dorothy Howell Rodham. She grew up in Park Ridge, Illinois, a suburb of Chicago, with her two younger brothers.

In 1969, she graduated from Wellesley College with honors and gave the class commencement speech. Hillary enrolled in Yale Law School, where she met Bill Clinton. They began dating soon after they met. In 1972, she testified before a hearing of the Democratic National Convention Platform Committee in Boston, Massachusetts, for the party to extend civil and political rights to children. She received her law degree in 1973 and accepted a position with the Children's Defense Fund in Cambridge, Massachusetts.

In 1974, she accepted a teaching position at the University of Arkansas Law School, where Bill Clinton was also a teacher. The following year, in August, Clinton purchased a house in Fayetteville that Hillary had admired, and he proposed. They were married two months later.

In 1980, a daughter, Chelsea Victoria, was born. At the time of the 1996 election, she was in her last year at the Sidwell Friends School, a private Quaker-run school in Washington, D.C.

In 1992, after Clinton was elected president, she headed a committee to reform the nation's health care system. The recommendations of her committee were rejected by Congress. She became the first First Lady to have an office in the West Wing of the White House, where the senior staff members of the president work. She also is the first lawyer to become First Lady. In 1996, she published *It Takes a Village and Other Lessons Children Teach Us.*

THE ARKANSAS GOVERNOR'S MANSION

1800 Center Street • Little Rock, Arkansas 72206 • Tel: (501) 376-6884

Among the proudest possessions of the Governor's Mansion is a 62-piece silver service located in the dining room. It was originally given to the battleship Arkansas *by the people of the State of Arkansas. After the battleship was decommissioned, it was donated to the mansion. The service includes a large punch bowl, which was cast from 3,000 silver dollars that were donated by Arkansas school children.* (Courtesy The Arkansas Governor's Mansion.)

Located off I-30. Take Second Street Exit to Center Street. Contact site for operating hours and dates. Tours available. No admission fee. Handicapped accessible. Administered by the State of Arkansas.

The two-story brick mansion, built in 1950 at a cost of $197,000, is located on an eight-acre site that was formerly owned by the Arkansas School for the Blind. Bricks from the school were used in the construction of the mansion. Two cottages, located on each side of the main building, are used as living quarters for the residing governor's security force and for visiting state guests and their families.

The interior contains Samuel F.B. Morse's portrait of James Miller, the first governor of Arkansas, which hangs above the fireplace in the living room.

In 1978, Bill and Hillary Clinton moved into the mansion. They lived there for two years. He lost his bid for reelection in 1980. The Clintons then purchased a house on Midland Avenue in the Pulaski Heights section of Little Rock. In 1982, he was reelected as governor and remained in the mansion until 1990, when he announced his candidacy for president.

RICHARD M. NIXON

Sallie G. Randolph's *Richard M. Nixon, President* (Walker, 1989) is an excellent general biography. Peter C. Ripley's *Richard Nixon* (Chelsea House, 1987) provides a thoughtful analysis of his entire political career. *Richard Nixon: Rise and Fall of a President* by Rebecca Larsen (Watts, 1991) is a well-researched biography of the only man to resign from the presidency. Although it is not a true biography, see Fred J. Cook's *Crimes of Watergate* (Watts, 1981) for a clear and concise analysis of the Watergate break-in and coverup. (For junior and senior high school.)

Carl Bernstein's *All The President's Men* (Simon & Schuster, 1974) and *The Final Days* by Bob Woodward (Simon & Schuster, 1976) tell the story of the Watergate scandal. Although not biographies, they both offer insight into Nixon's character and actions. *The Memoirs of Richard Nixon* by Richard Nixon (Grosset & Dunlap, 1978) offers a self-portrait along with a candid analysis of his strengths and weaknesses. The definitive biography is Stephen E. Ambrose's three-volume set *Nixon* (Simon & Schuster, 1987, 1989, 1991). Joan Hoff's *Nixon Reconsidered* (Basic Books, 1994) recounts some of his successes and attempts to put his presidency into perspective. *Pat Nixon: The Untold Story* by Julie N. Eisenhower (Simon & Schuster, 1986) offers much insight into the life of Pat Nixon, especially during her husband's presidency. Lester David's *The Lonely Lady of San Clemente* (Crowell, 1978) is another excellent biography of the First Lady. (For high school and adult.)

GERALD R. FORD

David R. Collins's *Gerald R. Ford* (Garrett Educational Corp., 1990) is a very good introductory biography. *Gerald R. Ford, President* by Sallie G. Randolph (Walker, 1987) is an excellent biography of the only man to become president without having been elected. (For junior and senior high school.)

Gerald R. Ford's *A Time to Heal* (Harper & Row, 1979) is a well-written autobiography that deals in a straightforward manner with his personal and his political lives and the tough choices he had to make. *Time and Chance* by James Cannor (HarperCollins, 1994) is a very informative and balanced biography that discusses the constitutional crisis created by Nixon's resignation and Ford's efforts to restore personal integrity to the presidency. Two books by Betty Ford (with Chris Chase) are *The Times of My Life* (Harper & Row, 1978) and *Betty, A Glad Awakening* (Doubleday, 1987). They deal with her personal tragedies and her triumph over cancer and substance abuse. Both are interesting and informative. (For high school and adult.)

JIMMY CARTER

Ed Slavin's *Jimmy Carter* (Chelsea House, 1989) is a well-written general introductory biography. *Jimmy Carter, President* by Betsy C. Smith (Walker, 1986) is an excellent biography, providing a well-balanced look at Carter. (For junior and senior high school.)

Jimmy Carter: In Search of the Great White House by Betty Glad (Norton, 1980) provides an analysis of his personal and political lives. The strengths and weaknesses of his administration are also discussed. Patrick Anderson's *Electing Jimmy Carter* (Louisiana State University Press, 1994) describes Jimmy Carter as both a complex person and a politician during and after his campaign for the nation's highest office. Rosalynn Carter's *First Lady from Plains* (Houghton Mifflin, 1984) is a well-done autobiography of a woman who fulfilled her dreams beyond expectation. *Everything to Gain* by Jimmy and Rosalynn Carter (Random House, 1987) presents a warm and unpretentious account of their life after the presidency and their adjustment to private life. (For high school and adult.)

RONALD REAGAN

John Devaney's *Ronald Reagan, President* (Walker, 1990) is a good, well-balanced introductory biography. Rebecca Larsen's *Ronald Reagan* (Watts, 1994) reviews his early life, his acting career, and his political life. (For junior and senior high school.)

For an in-depth portrait of his pregovernment years, see *Early Reagan* by Anne Edwards (Morrow, 1987). Robert Dallek's *Ronald Reagan: The Politics of Symbolism* (Harvard University Press, 1984) is well researched and well written, but it covers only a portion of his first term as president. *Ronald Reagan: His Life Story in Pictures* by Stanley P. Friedman (Dodd, Mead, 1986) is a well-done photo album of his life, accompanied by a solid narrative. *President Reagan, The Role of a Lifetime* by Lou Cannon (Simon & Schuster, 1991) is a meticulously researched biography with an emphasis on his presidency. *My Turn* by Nancy Reagan with William Novak (Random House, 1989) provides interesting reminiscences of the Reagans' personal and political lives. Peter Hannaford's *The*

Reagans: A Political Portrait (Coward-McCann, 1983) is a joint biography that presents insight into the 1980 political convention, the campaign, and Reagan's management style. (For high school and adult.)

GEORGE BUSH

George Sullivan's *George Bush* (Julian Messner, 1989) is a well-balanced introductory biography. *George H. W. Bush* by Rebecca Stefoff (Garrett Educational Corp., 1991) is an excellent general biography; however, it does not cover his full term as president. (For junior and senior high school.)

Flight of the Avenger by Joe Hyams (Harcourt Brace Jovanovich, 1991) is a readable and well-documented account of his wartime service in the U.S. Navy. It also includes his courtship of Barbara Pierce. Fitzhugh Green's *George Bush: An Intimate Portrait* (Hippocrine Books, 1989) is a good analysis of his early formative years and goes through his first year as president. *The Bush Presidency: First Appraisals,* edited by Colin Campbell (Chatham House, 1991), offers a wide range of perspectives on his presidency at midterm. Pamela Kilian's *Barbara Bush: A Biography* (St. Martin's Press, 1992) is a highly readable biography of the extremely popular First Lady. *Barbara Bush: A Memoir* by Barbara Bush (St. Martin's Press, 1995) is a lively recounting of her life from childhood to First Lady that offers an insider's look into politics at the highest levels. (For high school and adult.)

BILL CLINTON

Michael D. Cole's *Bill Clinton: United States President* (Enslow Press, 1994) is a balanced introductory biography. (For junior and senior high school.)

Charles F. Allen's *The Comeback Kid* (Carol Publishing Group, 1992) is a well-researched and well-written analysis of his life before the presidency. *On The Make: The Rise of Bill Clinton* by Meredith L. Oakley (Regnery Publishers, 1994) is an excellent comprehensive biography covering his rise to political power in Arkansas and in Washington. *First in His Class* by David Maraniss (Simon & Schuster, 1995) offers a solid, well-researched analysis of Clinton and describes his personal and political strengths and weaknesses. George Carpozi's *Clinton Confidential* (Emery Dalton Books, 1995) is a candid unauthorized biography of Bill and Hillary Rodham Clinton. (For high school and adult.)

First Lady: The Story of Hillary Rodham Clinton by Aaron Boyd (Morgan Reynolds, 1994) presents a well-done introduction to the First Lady. (For junior high school.)

Donnie Radcliffe's *Hillary Rodham Clinton* (Warner Books, 1993) is an excellent biography of the First Lady that emphasizes her life before the White House. (For high school and adult.)

at a glance . . .

President	Volume	President	Volume	President	Volume
George Washington	1	James Buchanan	3	Calvin Coolidge	5
John Adams	1	Abraham Lincoln	3	Herbert Hoover	5
Thomas Jefferson	1	Andrew Johnson	3	Franklin D. Roosevelt	6
James Madison	1	Ulysses S. Grant	3	Harry S. Truman	6
James Monroe	1	Rutherford B. Hayes	4	Dwight D. Eisenhower	6
John Quincy Adams	2	James A. Garfield	4	John F. Kennedy	6
Andrew Jackson	2	Chester A. Arthur	4	Lyndon B. Johnson	6
Martin Van Buren	2	Grover Cleveland	4	Richard M. Nixon	7
William Henry Harrison	2	Benjamin Harrison	4	Gerald R. Ford	7
John Tyler	2	William McKinley	4	Jimmy Carter	7
James K. Polk	2	Theodore Roosevelt	5	Ronald Reagan	7
Zachary Taylor	3	William Howard Taft	5	George Bush	7
Millard Fillmore	3	Woodrow Wilson	5	Bill Clinton	7
Franklin Pierce	3	Warren G. Harding	5		